The Cup of Wonder

The Cup of Wonder

Lloyd John Oglivie

BAKER BOOK HOUSE
Grand Rapids, Michigan 49506

To Andrew
Son, friend, and brother in Christ

Contents

Introduction

When I was asked to compile a book of communion meditations, I responded reluctantly at first. My messages in preparation for the Lord's Supper are deeply personal times of loving conversation with my people. How could I reproduce for the reader's eye the intimacy and closeness I feel when I stand behind the Table and lead my family of faith into the holy of holies of the sacrament? Would the depth of my pastor's heart come through? Could the book be something more than preacher's rhetoric and expositor's insight?

I knew that if I sat down to write a series of meditations specifically for publication, my desire for written perfection would dominate the effort, and the result would miss the authenticity of the actual celebration of communion. For that reason, I agreed to have the tapes of the communion meditations I have delivered at my Hollywood Church transcribed and edited for publication. The style of the spoken word has been maintained throughout to give the reader the feel of the actual messages. I am indebted to my good friend Mary Tregenza for her faithful transposition onto the written page of what I both felt and said in those tender moments when I shared the communion with my beloved people.

On Communion Sundays, the Lord's Table is moved down to the lower steps of the chancel, next to the people. The service is profoundly relational. Each aspect of the service is shared by the people. The greeting of one another in Christ's name, the assurance of pardon after confession, the sharing of the peace, the words of institution, and the blessing at the benediction are all given first by the pastors and then by the people to each other. A great sanctuary seating hundreds of people of all ages and backgrounds becomes an intimate Upper Room. Our Lord is there in power and love, forgiveness and the hope of new beginnings. The music combines the traditional majesty of praise anthems and the more contemporary folk and hymn tunes. The order of the service is carefully planned to help our people to get in touch with the Savior, themselves, and each other. Praise flows into confession. Our brokenness is healed by prayers of intercession and supplication. The congregation joins hands in singing "We Are One in the Bond of Love."

Then it's time for a brief meditation on the meaning of the sacrament in the context of the people's needs. On each Communion Sunday, I try to take an aspect of the grace of our Lord Jesus and relate it to the frustrations, hopes, and hurts of contemporary Christians who are trying to live the adventure of the new life faithfully and obediently. I believe that Calvin was right when he said that the sacrament becomes meaningless repetition unless the Word is exposited before the people partake of the sacred elements.

The greatest need of my people is for the living Christ. We need his indwelling power and gifts more than anything or anyone else. Paul was right. "Christ in you, the hope of glory!"

Holy Communion is that very special time when we receive him. Taking the sacrament is our awesome time to receive Christ's living presence. He is faithful to his promise. He enters our minds so we can think his thoughts; he floods our emotions so we can love each other as he has loved us; he captivates our wills so that we can respond to his guidance; and he penetrates every fibre of our bodies with healing and health. His amazing grace is mediated and we are free to love him, ourselves, and each other.

I sincerely hope that these messages will be helpful to you in your own daily communion with our Lord. His indwelling Spirit is constantly seeking a new and deeper relationship with us. Our conversations with him in prayer can be our daily, Holy Communion. I pray that each of these meditations will lead you into his presence and then back to your responsibilities and concerns with new freedom and joy.

1

The Feast
of Freedom

Jeremiah 52:31-34

Let me dramatize for you what it means for me to take communion.

Picture for a moment the sumptuous beauty of that dining hall in Babylon. Sense the array of kings. Let the moving images of the colorful pageantry, the perilous protocol, the dazzling splendor loop through the gate of your mind.

Evil-merodach sits at the head of this magnificent company. From an obscure door at the side of the room, a slight figure enters. He is stooped. His psyche, his deep inner self is also bowed, obviously the result of years of imprisonment. He has bypassed the fanfare of an entrance because he wants no recognition, only a seat at the edge of the splendor. It is enough that he is free, that his bowed head has been lifted up after thirty-seven years.

A stir ripples across the great chamber as the new visitor is intercepted. Instead of being placed at the side of the banquet table, the frail figure is called forth and given a seat above all the kings in Babylon!

Thirty-seven years before, Nebuchadnezzar had swept down on Jerusalem, taking the queen mother and Jehoiachin off to Babylon. After an insurrection, Jehoiachin was banished to solitary confinement. Year after year he languished there until Evil-merodach came to the throne. One of the new king's first acts was to go to the prison, lift up the head of Jehoiachin, and whisper these drenchingly beautiful words, "You are free!"

Not only did the king take him out of prison, he invited him to put off his prison garb and dine at the royal table. What serendipitous grace! What a fantastic portion of Scripture as the basis of Holy Communion!

"So Jehoiachin put off his prison garments. And ... he dined regularly at the king's table."

This is what it means for me to break the bread and take the cup. It means laying aside my prison garb to dine with the King. It means that I am set free to be the man I was created to be. To live life as it was meant to be lived.

And it means that I now invite you to this incredible feast of freedom.

What is it that binds you and keeps you from being a free man or a free woman? What memories of the past, what relationships of the present, what uncertainties of the future keep you bound?

What cycle of condemnation are you locked into? What inflexibility, what habit patterns keep you incarcerated in the prison of life? Why is it that you react in certain situations the way you do and find it so difficult to grow to be the liberated, unique person you were meant to be?

The living Christ moves among us, and our bound and imprisoned spirits are suddenly lifted. He takes hold of us, lifts us up. Tenderly we see him face to face!

Suddenly we are experiencing communion with him. In his presence, the prison garb no longer fits. It binds. It distresses. In such a moment, we want more than anything else to be a free person.

Paul said, "Now the Lord is the Spirit, and where the Spirit of the Lord is, there is freedom!" (2 Corinthians 3:17)

It is the Spirit who comes within us as we reach out for these symbols of costly grace. And as we eat of the bread and drink of the cup, he comes to live in us, and from within us he does a magnificent thing.

From deep below the level of words, he assures us that in spite of it all, we are forgiven. That whatever distracts us and gives us a sense of guilt or uncertainty when we come into his presence can be washed away. And he reminds us that he can take the raw material of our future and shape it into something significant and splendid.

We can never earn a right place with God. It is by grace that we come to this Table. To those of us who would cower at the sight of the banquet hall, who fear to come to the table, let alone stand with the kings, he says, "Friend, come up higher. Come sit with me for I have released you from your own prison. I love you. I want you to be a free person."

THE CUP OF WONDER

I invite you to come to this feast of freedom, to come and dine with the Lord and his people as a liberated person. For freedom Christ has set us free!
Amen.

2
Jesus Must Go to Come

John 16:7-16
Luke 24:50-53

What a paradox! Could it possibly be true? The record says that he—Jesus—departed, and they—the disciples—returned to Jerusalem with great joy.

How could it be?

Gone now were the days of excitement and challenge. Memory's gallery alone would be their sanctuary of comfort in which to recapture the unspeakable joy of meeting and following Jesus. Now only in their mind's eye could they see the lame leaping with joy, the deaf able to hear, the blind seeing anew in Jesus' healing, liberating presence.

In the quiet solemnity of their own company, they would have to sort out the fact of human hatred and the anguishing details of Gethsemane and Calvary. They would have to face life without his physical, resurrected presence, and yet they returned to Jerusalem rejoicing. How could this be?

"Parting is such sweet sorrow." Not so, Shakespeare!

Remember the heartache and anguish when waiting

for the gangplank to be lifted, the train to begin to move, or the flight to be called? We can feel again the despair of the wrenching of deep human bonds. Our ever-faithful memory takes us to a bedside and the pain of watching a loved one receding, being eaten alive with a virulent cancerous poison. We relive the torture of parent's suffering or children taken. We remember and we cry out for the mercy of the subconscious to close the door against feelings we had hoped would never again stalk the hallways of our minds.

And yet the disciples returned rejoicing. How can this be?

But look more closely at the facts. Come to terms with our text and you will be confronted with one of the most profound paradoxes of the Scriptures, "It is to your advantage that I go away."

The disciples' joy was rooted in the bitter experience that Jesus must go in order to come. At first, with hostility and fear, they had resisted the possibility of his leaving. That was long before the Ascension when they were still bound by preconceptions about the kingdom being ushered in with massive social and religious reverberations. But the same minds that could not encompass the truth that it could ever be to their advantage for Jesus to leave them were now rejoicing. And this is why.

When Jesus said that his departure would be expedient for them, he disclosed two tremendous truths. One involves the plan of God, the other the nature of man. Jesus unveiled the secret of how we shall grow and declared the omnipresence of God.

Jesus knew that his disciples would not attain spiritual maturity as long as he was with them. There is a spiritual secret here. He left them because he wanted them to grow up. So it is for us. In the ebb and flow of life, Jesus will leave us to prompt us on to new growth and to prepare us to receive him in a different and deeper way.

Up to this point the method of spiritual direction had only been preliminary—precept and visible example. His strange words told them now that there is a better education in discipleship than that which can be supplied by a visible master whose will can never be misunderstood. From now on the braver and more perfect disciple would be one who walks in the creative interface of faith.

Jesus said, "Have you believed because you have seen me? Blessed are those who have not seen and yet believe."

The training of the disciples had only begun. Repeatedly they had made the mistake of using what little insight and wisdom they had gained as a principle instead of developing new trust in him. Each time he disappeared, they were thunderstruck with fear. Until they found him again, praying in a mountain retreat or coming to them on a tumultuous sea, their hearts would pound with childish anxiety. They could not grow up alone. Jesus nurtured them each step of the way.

We are not unlike those disciples in our reluctance to grow. We come to a point of security in our spiritual growth and we desperately block out any invading thought or theory that would challenge us to think about who we really are and what our true inner relationship to Christ is. We have an infinite capacity for sidestepping challenges which demand new insight, commitment, and reorientation of thought.

Who of us has not experienced the dark night of the soul when little reason can be found in life? It would not take a long memory for any one of us to remember when life pressed in upon us and we wondered if we could withstand the temptation to jettison faith or hope. In such a moment, we realize how shallow our relationship with the Lord really is, and we are driven to deeper trust, study, and fellowship.

Jesus pulls the props out from under our preconceptions and drops the bottom out of our satisfied religion. We should remember in that moment of loneliness that he is preparing us to receive him in new depth and power.

Our Lord uses the tragedies of life. None of us is exempt. Burns was right:

> If every man's internal care
> Were written on his brow,
> How many who our envy share
> Would have our pity now?

Internal care can break or build—atomize or galvanize—our faith.

The sovereign power of Christ is exercised when he takes tragedy and uses it to help us grow. Jesus' torture and tragic death brought the disciples to an honest realization of how evil and devious human nature really was. All childish human aspirations to bring in a kingdom of their own faithful goodness died at the crucifixion.

It's all in the attitude we take in these dungeons of

despair. Can Jesus use this? What is your message, Lord? Samuel Rutherford, the great Scottish saint, found the answer: "Fool that I was not to know that the messages of God are not read through the envelope in which they are enclosed." We cannot see it at first, but ultimately it is revealed that most of our significant growth comes in hours like these.

Blaise Pascal wrote the most profound words I have ever read on the ultimate power of Christ to teach us in the midst of difficulty. He wrote to a friend:

> If we follow this precept and if we regard this event not as an effect of chance, not as a fatal necessity of nature, but as a result indispensable, inevitable, just and holy, of a decree of His providence, conceived from all eternity to be executed at such an hour and in such a manner, we shall adore in humble silence the impenetrable loftiness of His secrets; we shall venerate the sanctities of His decrees, we shall bless the acts of providence and submit our will to that of God Himself. We shall wish with Him and for Him the thing He has willed in us and for us from all eternity.

When Hezekiah received the letter from Sennacherib's lieutenant threatening the destruction of Jerusalem, he went into the Temple and literally spread the letter out before the Lord and asked for his will to be done. This is the answer for these times of despair. Acquaint him with the matter from your point of view and surrender for his will to be done.

Can we say with the Psalmist, "It is good that I have been afflicted"? We need to wrestle like Jacob until we are given a blessing from the angel of growth who pushes us on. The blessing is Jesus Christ coming to us in a new way.

That's why the disciples were rejoicing on the way back to Jerusalem. They had finally progressed to where they could accept the second part of Jesus' statement, "If I do not go away, the Comforter will not come to you; but if I go, I will send him to you." The Holy Spirit would be sent to them by Jesus as the omnipresent, universal Lord. Jesus had completed his incarnate life and soon he would return as indwelling Lord. He returned to the Father in order to reign over history as the universal prophet, priest, and king of all life.

"It is to your advantage that I go away...."

Jesus' death seemed to be the end of all he affirmed to be true. His resurrection proclaimed the final word, however. Jesus of Nazareth, whose death could not contradict his life and whose resurrection validated his death, was ascended to be available to the hearts and minds of a new creation.

That quivering little band of men joyously heading for Jerusalem and the Upper Room would be the beginning of a new breed of men and women: The nucleus of a chosen, holy race to live out and proclaim to the world a new kind of life whose signature was love, freedom, peace, and power.

Paul caught the vision of it all in Ephesians 1:19-23.

What is the immeasurable greatness of his power in us who believe, according to the working of his great might which he accomplished in Christ when he raised him from the dead and made him sit at his right hand in the heavenly places, far above all rule and authority and power and dominion, and above every name that is named, not only in this age but also in that which is to come; and he has put all things under his feet and has made him the head over all things for the church, which is his body, the fulness of him who fills all in all.

When Jesus returned to his disciples, he returned in the power of the Holy Spirit, to indwell them and enable them to be all that he had promised. With him as the image of what life could be, the disciples went out into the world to do the things he had done. The promise of Jesus recorded in John 14 came to life. "Because I go to the Father," Jesus said, the things his disciples would ask in his name would be done. He would continue to do what he had done—only now he would do it through his people.

God, who does not need us, has, because of his greatness, called us to be channels of his Spirit. As he invested his power in a nation and then revealed his love in a Son, it is now his strategy of redemption to live in and through his people.

The divine experiment has not failed. The living Lord is here. Resisting imprisonment in a single frame of history through us. Waiting to reveal himself to us in the breaking of bread. Seeking to love through us. To overcome evil through us. To heal through us.

Will you recognize him at the feast of remembrance?

Realize that the hands that pass the bread are his hands? Acknowledge that the hands that raise the cup to your lips are his hands?

Jesus has spoken to us of our nature and God's majesty. We are encouraged to live with new trust and abandon. The Lord has ascended and he is here.

Praise God!

3

Communion in the Kingdom

Luke 22:14-20;
Matthew 26:29

Does God play favorites?

Are the blessings of his love, power, and peace available only to an elite few? Why do some persons seem to experience them and others never know their reality?

Before us is the Communion Table. We have responded to the invitation to come to receive the sacrament in remembrance of his broken body and shed blood. We will affirm again this memorial in time and space of our God's supreme expression of his never-changing love.

Now some of us will leave this service refreshed, released, and rejoicing. Others will leave unmoved, uninspired, and unchanged. What makes the difference?

Perhaps one had a better night's rest or less on his mind? Or fewer troubles at home, at the office, or with his friends? I doubt it. Perhaps one is simply in better emotional health than another. I also doubt that. The difference between the two is that one has fulfilled the qualification for communion. The others have not.

Holy Communion is the feast of the kingdom. This is the necessary preparation for communion. Jesus said: "I tell you I shall not drink again of this fruit of the vine until that day when I drink it new with you in my Father's kingdom" (Matthew 26:29).

When Jesus spoke these words in his closed-door briefing on the night of his betrayal, he was giving his disciples a promise, a stipulation, and a cause for rejoicing. He promised that he would return, that he would sup with them again, but next time it would be in another context—the Father's kingdom. The most important aspect of his statement is that the feast he established could not have meaning unless it was celebrated new ... with him ... within his Father's kingdom.

The kingdom of God is the sovereign rule of God in the lives of men—and through them in every phase of life. We have based our thesis on the Psalmist's words: "The earth is the Lord's and the fulness thereof, the world and those who dwell therein" (Psalm 24:1).

All of life belongs to God, but the kingdom of God exists wherever individuals affirm this and live with every phase of their lives under the lordship of Christ. Holy Communion is the feast of the kingdom. Unless we are consciously seeking God's rule in all things, this feast is empty and void.

The qualifications are quite clear in this traditional invitation to communion:

> Ye who do truly and earnestly repent of your sins, and are in love and charity with your neighbors, and intend to lead a new life, following the commandments of God, and walking

from henceforth in his holy ways: Draw near
with faith, and take this Holy Sacrament to your
comfort, and make your humble confession to
Almighty God.

There are three definite aspects to this challenging
invitation. They are: repentance; love and charity with
neighbors; and the desire to live a new life under the
sovereignty of God.

Repentance is the key which unlocks the door of the
kingdom. Jesus recognized it as the first step. "The
Kingdom of God is at hand; repent, and believe in the
gospel" (Mark 1:15).

Repent ... believe. How closely these words are related. The gospel is the good news of God's love and
forgiveness made real in Jesus Christ. Repentance and
belief are man's reaction and response to God's exciting
revelation in Christ—that God is Ruler of creation and
wishes to make this operative in the world through the
free will of persons who allow his rule to exist in every
level of their lives!

It is through the act of repentance that a person turns
from self-rule to God's rule. God will continue to rule in
the world whether we like it or not, but his rule becomes creative in us only as we repent of the sin of
self-rule and are governed by God-control. Every sin in
our life is a manifestation of this self-dominion.

The profoundest level of spiritual depth perceived in
the Old Testament is not the offer of man's righteousness to God but his contrition. In the New Testament,
there is an integral connection between repentance and
faith or belief. To repent is to turn, and a man must

make a radical turn from self-rule to God. Faith or belief is the definite release of the control of our lives to God. It is the encounter with God that produces the response of repentance and belief rather than repentance and belief bringing about the response of God.

The second ingredient of communion in the kingdom is relational. It involves the quality of our relationships in the complex forms and structure of communal life. Are we in love and charity with our neighbors? This sacred sacrament and these power-packed words will be a mockery if you have not allowed the kingdom to penetrate the relationships of your life. Jesus said: "If you are offering your gift at the altar, and there remember that your brother has something against you, leave your gift there before the altar and go; first be reconciled to your brother, and then come and offer your gift" (Matthew 5:23, 24).

Jesus clearly proclaimed that faithfulness and broken relationships could not mix. We cannot participate in this spiritual feast with meaning if we have frustrations, fears, hostility, and hatred against others. Love and charity are two closely related words—some translations of the Scriptures use them interchangeably. Love must have expression in overt acts of charity. We love in general but abhor the specific. God abhors the general and rubs our nose in the specific. He was never more specific for the sickness of the world than he was in Jesus Christ.

When will we free the channels of God's unmerited, unearned love to others? It's a condition of communion.

The third aspect suggested in the invitation to communion is this: Do we "intend to lead a new life, following the commandments of God, and walking from henceforth in his holy ways"? This question deals with the future.

Praise God, our faith is a hope of new beginnings! We are invited to start fresh. The failures of each day can be washed clean. We can be new every morning rather than dragging the broken wings of past failures into each new day. Note, however, that the statement deals with intention and not performance. We are motivated by the intention of our wills deep within us. We often wonder why we find it so difficult to act in accordance with our best image of ourselves. It is because we do not intend—will—to do it deep within. God can take our intention and give us power to follow through.

A new life! How exciting this thought is. Advertisers say that the word "new" is the most potent in our language. We are encouraged to want the new and different. But a new life? Is this possible? A new relationship of peace with yourself? A new love life where mutual love exists? A new feeling of excitement about your job? A new level of honesty with your friends?

This touches us where we all ache and yearn. How we long to be liberated from ennui and boredom. How wonderful to be new and different. The hope of the kingdom of God is exactly this. We are called into a new life under the rule of God.

The problem of dreary sameness is not in our external life. The problem is within. Our intentions are wrong. They are still programmed to perpetuate old patterns and relationships. "Remember not the former things," the Lord urged Israel through Isaiah. "Behold I am doing a new thing; now it springs forth, do you not perceive it?" (Isaiah 43:18, 19). Something new and greater than anything they had ever realized, would come through the messianic age.

David prayed in Psalm 51:10, "Create in me a clean heart, O God, and put a new and right spirit within me." Ezekiel spoke of this same reality when he said, prophesying for God, "A new heart will I give you, and a new spirit will I put within you; and I will take out of your flesh the heart of stone and give you a heart of flesh" (Ezekiel 36:26).

Jesus Christ, who fulfilled the promises of the prophets for a new life, also promised his disciples that he would not drink the fruit of the vine until he drank it new in his Father's kingdom. Jesus promised a new covenant meaning a new relationship with himself. He would return each time they broke bread and drank wine together!

To long to live in the new life is a preparation for communion. Jesus' words to the disciples that he would not drink of the fruit of the vine until he drank it new in his Father's kingdom were immediate words of high comfort, the tryst of a beloved for dark hours ahead. They were also words of joyous anticipation and promise. The kingdom was on its way! No one could stop it now! His death and resurrection would only seal its victory.

We come to the Lord's Table in the joy of this victory. God has won. The resources of God's power are ours. Come, let us celebrate. The kingdom has come and we have been asked to live in it!

And Jesus Christ is here to drink of the cup new with us!

4
The Elijah Complex

1 Kings 19:1-14

There is a kind of grimness which grips the people of God. It comes when they take themselves too seriously and fail to take God seriously enough. When they lose sight of God's sovereignty. Are overwhelmed by the indefatigability of evil. And forget they are not alone.

This is the sickness of the Elijah complex.

It displaces the joy of the Christian faith with the self-assertiveness of an obsession. It begins with doubt, spreads into disappointment, and immobilizes in despair.

This spiritual malaise is named for its founder, and its cure is discernible in the way God dealt with that man's life. Healing is present for us today. It waits for our honest cry for forgiveness and wholeness as we come to the Lord's Table.

It was immediately following his victory over the priests of Baal on Mount Carmel that Elijah was struck a blow that almost destroyed him. Ahab's recounting to Jezebel of the massacre of her prophets invoked bitter abjurations on her cowering husband and fierce vindictiveness on this dark, fanatic prophet. Her anger boiled hot: "So may the gods do to me, and more also, if I do not make your life as the life of one of them by this time tomorrow." Elijah was worried.

It was unbelievable. This unflinching, unflappable man who had fought for Jehovah and won was worried. This man who had prophesied drought and enemy crops withered; who prayed for rain and it came in a rush of blessing; who snatched the Phoenician widow's boy from death; who stood before kings and was not afraid; who had confronted the richly vested, royally maintained Baal priests and in spite of their orgiastic leapings and self-mutilations had put their sun god to shame under his own burning rays; who had kept pace with Ahab's chariot steed in a downpour of rain for which he had prayed—this man was worried!

More than that, he was drenched with despair. In the face of the indominatable image of evil in Jezebel and the indefatigable force of evil in the world, Elijah turned on his heel and ran for his life. He didn't stop running for twelve tormented hours.

He collapsed finally in utter exhaustion under a broom tree. He cried: "It is enough now, O Lord, take away my life; for I am no better than my fathers." Later he said, "I, even I only, am left; and they seek my life, to take it away." He fell asleep in utter despair.

At the moment of victory, something broke within this man and he became the cause of his own defeat. Does that sound familiar?

Have you ever found that after some personal or social achievement you have a drab, dry spell? Have you ever chalked up an exciting victory over some habit only to find that you have fallen into a more serious and subtle one? It's the Elijah complex. A sudden sickness of the soul.

What were the elements in this complicated compound? First, we suspect that Elijah was profoundly naive. He had that limiting concept of the spiritual which led him to believe that all evil was localized in the priests of Baal. He was astounded to learn that the Mount Carmel victory had barely scratched the surface. Jezebel, the sensual prophetess, was still in power. Was Mount Carmel anything more than a deplorable failure?

Have you ever felt that way? Have you ever worked hard to establish some new program, stamp out some evil in the community, overcome some personal problem—only to find that the sickness has broken through in some new place? We can understand Elijah's frustration.

Another facet in the Elijah complex was that he deeply wanted to be adequate as God's man in Israel. There was so much to do and he had hardly begun to touch the need. To mobilize the reform. To savor the wonder of being in God's service. But how humiliating when he didn't measure up.

I find in myself and in no small number of you, the abrasive guilt of unfulfilled promises and unespoused causes. Wouldn't it be wonderful to get away from it all? To escape from reality under a broom tree?

Another component of the Elijah complex was his lack of courage when evil was personal—incarnate in an evil woman. He could deal with evil in a nation, or in a cult of priests, or in an external principal. But when face to face with an evil woman whose name was the most feared in Israel, Elijah was not so different from all the rest. He could confront her evil cause, but he could not deal with her.

Are you beguiled by power in a person? Do your eloquent protestations evaporate on your lips in the presence of some person who actually personifies the evil you protest? Can you stand and say what you think when your opportunity comes?

Elijah could not. Even after he had disarmed Jezebel so completely that her only weapon was a vain threat, he turned and ran. He could have destroyed her, but he was afraid of her. Poor Elijah.

It is significant that the psychological factors which produced the Elijah complex had physical and emotional roots. Elijah had worked without care for himself for some days. After he had raced Ahab to Jezreel, he had staggered over the ninety-five miles to Beersheba and then a day's journey beyond that. Extreme physical exhaustion is always the result of working for God rather than allowing God to work through us. The effect of our omnicompetence rather than his omnipotence.

Instead of a temple of God's Spirit, Elijah had made his body a tomb of his own self-perpetuating ego. The result was a kind of early megalomania, a telltale symptom of an Elijah complex. He thought he alone was left as a faithful man in Israel. "Listen, God, it's only me and thee left now!"

And in that order!

We express the same thing in our homes. Have you grown in the conviction that you alone keep the faith in your family? Are you God's last hope of getting husband or wife to church? Do you feel you represent something your family doesn't have but can get only through you? Do you ever get downright grim about it?

How about church? Do you suspect that you and God alone are being faithful to the religious heritage you so value? Ever feel you are all alone in keeping your church pure? That everyone else is believing too little, trusting themselves too much, spending on the wrong things, voting for the wrong people? Do you secretly wish you could straighten them out?

How does God deal with the Elijah complex? The first thing he did was to give him rest and food. God is very practical. He created the laws by which we live and our healing begins by our observance of them.

> The innocent sleep,
> Sleep that binds up the raveled sleeve of care,...
> Balm of hurt minds, great nature's second
> course,
> Chief nourisher in life's feast.
> (*Macbeth*, Act II, Sc. ii, l. 36)

Elijah had to join the human race and stop thinking he was god over Israel. God knew what the Greek tragedian articulated later, that Elijah's "sleeping mind was bright with eyes." As the Spirit of God penetrated Elijah's unconscious mind, his sleep was not an escape but an encounter.

A simple instruction usually breaks the Elijah complex. Oswald Chambers said:

> The angel did not give Elijah a vision, or explain the Scriptures to him, or do anything remark-

35

able. He told Elijah to do the most ordinary thing—to get up and eat. If we were never depressed we should not be alive. It is the nature of a crystal never to be depressed. A human being is capable of depression, otherwise there would be no capacity for exaltation. There are things that are calculated to depress, things that are of the nature of death; and in taking an estimate of yourself, always take into account the capacity for depression.

When the Spirit of God comes he does not give us visions, he tells us to do the most ordinary things conceivable. Depression is apt to turn us away from the ordinary commonplace things of God's creation, but whenever God comes, the inspiration is to do the most natural simple things—the things we would never have imagined God was in. And as we do them we find he is there. The inspiration which comes to us in this way is an initiative against depression; we have to do the next thing and do it in the inspiration of God. If we do a thing in order to overcome depression, we deepen the depression. But if the Spirit of God makes us feel intuitively that we must do the thing, and we do it, the depression is gone. Immediately we arise and obey, we enter on a higher plane of life.[1]

Now Elijah was given instructions to go to Horeb, the mount of God. There, half healed and unaware of what

[1] *My Utmost for His Highest*, Oswald Chambers. (New York: Dodd, Mead and Company, 1935), page 48.

God was up to, he hid away in a cave of escape. But God would not leave him alone, his wound only lightly healed. He must leave his cave for a manifestation of the central truth.

"What are you doing here, Elijah?" It was the basic, clarifying question and it was intensified by the display of God's power. First there was the great wind. Then there was the earthquake. Then there was the fire of lightning. Do you realize what is happening? The physical manifestations on which Elijah had depended for his experience of God were to no avail. God was not in any of these.

Then in the utter silence of Mount Horeb, God spoke—in a still, small voice. By this we understand that the Holy Spirit of God confirmed his presence within Elijah and spoke inaudibly through Elijah's thoughts and insight. Peace and power are the Spirit's gifts and can be found nowhere else. Elijah heard now because for the first time he was quiet enough to listen.

There are voices of inspiration, correction, and direction which we never hear because we do not listen. When we are quiet in the woods, sounds which we have never heard before become apparent. Rivers which flow beneath the ancient city of Shechem cannot be heard in the daytime above the noise of the bazaars in the narrow streets. When evening comes and the clamor dies away, you may hear the music of the buried streams.

So it is in the spiritual life. We have caught the art of being strenuous—"Whatever your hand finds to do, do it with your might"—and we have lost the art of being still—"Be still and know that I am God." I am frightened when I realize how little of God I know because I have been quiet so little. George Mattheson said, "There are tidings from the Eternal Spirit who is not far from any one of us; tidings that will come and go unnoticed unless we have won the grace of being still."

"What are you doing here, Elijah?" Up to this moment he was too depressed, too exhausted, too guilty to hear the question God had been asking. Now, in the gentle stillness, he heard and could answer.

This is the ministry of the Holy Spirit in our lives. In quietness he works on our character. In stillness he tempers our emotions, heals our frustration, clears the cloudy vision, and helps us to see things as they really are. We need these times of deep quiet in which the issues of life come really clear.

How often I have had the experience of the Spirit in quiet and how painful his helpful probing can be. "Lloyd, why do you have that attitude? Why do you resent that person? Why do you fear that situation? What *are* you doing here? What are *you* doing here? What are you *doing* here? What are you doing *here?*" Think of the many ways that question can be leveled.

Elijah's journey back to wholeness began with a simple response to this invitation: "Arise and eat because the journey is too great for you." A similar invitation is extended to us at the Lord's Table. There is no accident in the fact that our Lord first offered these symbols of new life to a company of grim, disillusioned, fear-ridden, ambitious men. He knew they could never make it alone without him. That's why he gave them the means of grace in the broken bread, to be made whole.

The Elijah Complex

"Eat ye all of it," Christ said. "This is my body ... broken for you." That alone can heal the Elijah complex and give us Christ confidence!

Are we willing to take the first step away from the grim grip of the mentalities and complexes that cripple and warp our psyches? In this simple response we may indeed enter a higher plane of life. In the quiet of our heart we are strengthened. We hear words of forgiveness. Words of courage. Words of hope. And then, through the thoughts and emotions of our quieted beings, we will be ready to hear simple words of direction.

Be still. God has something to say.

5
It's Time to Celebrate

Luke 15:11-32

I called a friend of mine in another denomination one day and his secretary answered the telephone. When I asked to speak to him, she said, "He can't come to the telephone now. He's celebrating!"

I said, "Well, I'm for that. But what is he celebrating at this hour of the morning?"

And she said, "He's celebrating Holy Communion."

I thought to myself, "What a wonderful description of the Holy Communion. A celebration of the broken body and the shed blood of Jesus Christ."

How many of you have awakened on a Communion Sunday and said, "Today I'm going to a celebration!"? How many of you, as you see the Lord's Table before you, have a sense of the excitement and the adventure of being at a great celebration?

Jesus said that knowing God and having fellowship with him was like a banquet. A feast. And when he described the inner experience of God's love at the feast, he described it as joy!

Joy is the identifiable outward manifestation of the inner experience of God's grace. In Greek, *chara* is the result of *charis* from within. It is when we know his power within that it spreads in a contagious, uncontainable joy outwardly. And to know and to live with the living God is like being at a celebration. It means coming to a great banquet. It means enjoying him—and each other.

There is no more poignant story in the New Testament than the story of the three prodigals. That's right, three.

I have given this passage of Scripture a new title because I don't believe this is only the parable of the prodigal son. It is the parable of three prodigals.

There are three definitions of prodigality, and each one wonderfully describes a major character in this parable and each of us. There is the younger son who took his inheritance and squandered it. Profligate squandering of wealth, time, or energy is one definition of prodigality.

But there's a second definition that fits the elder brother. There is a prodigality of use and a prodigality of disuse. There's a prodigality that squanders and a prodigality that hoards. There's a way of leaving the father and going into a far country, and there's a way of never leaving at all and still being in a far country. There's a far country of spirit in the father's household.

The third kind of prodigality is lavish giving. It is the excessive pouring forth of oneself and one's possessions in bountiful appreciation. And that's the description of the Father.

When Jesus wanted to describe what God was like he

pictured him as a father running down the hill to meet his son. That is the picture of God I want to keep before us as we prepare to celebrate.

Here is a profile of God that is freshly New Testament. We catch a glimmer of it in some of the prophets, but prior to Christ, man's religion was dominated by his efforts to please or placate God with right sacrifices, self-justifying rituals, and petulant perfectionism. The priests alone could go into the Holy of Holies. God was considered high and lifted up, beyond the reach of man's best efforts.

Do you recognize what a revolution Jesus began? What a tremendous metamorphosis of the idea of God in history he proclaimed? Not a God far away in the cloistral calm of the Holy of Holies, but a God who runs in search of his people!

I want to tell you that he is here, and that he is running in search of every one of us whose prodigality has been expressed in misuse or disuse of his gracious gifts.

Picture him running to you. You who have a feeling of brokenness and separation from him or anyone else. You whose memories burn hot with things you'd never say or do again—but you can't forget. You who say as you come to communion, "I have no right to be here. If the people beside me knew what I've done, I wouldn't dare come to this Table!"

My brothers and sisters, he runs to welcome you home. On your finger he puts a ring kept for a beloved child, and says, "You are my child and that will never change." He puts the robe around you that's kept for special guests. He puts shoes on your feet, a symbol of the fact that you're no longer a slave feeding the swine in the fields.

You are now his honored guest.

The same Lord who ended his suffering on the Cross with the words, "It is finished!" is the one who said at the conclusion of preparations for the banquet feast, "Come, for all is now ready."

And, oh, it is ready...

God is so ready for us at his Table. Ready with love and forgiveness. Ready with a new beginning, a new opportunity. But there are some of us here who are elder brothers and whose prodigality is the misuse of the gift of life. We've hoarded it. Kept it to ourselves.

It's strange, isn't it, how the returning prodigal sons eventually become elder brothers in the institutional church? It isn't long before we are standing at the very port of entry that we had to the Father, judging the people who want to come home to him.

There's no sin more serious than the sickness of not knowing you are sick. There's no need greater than the need of knowing your need. There's no arrogance quite like the arrogance of the elder brother who cannot sense the rhythms of God's Spirit yearning for the prodigal to come home.

To be so out of touch with the Father that you can't come in and dance at his feast is a terrible thing.

There are some people here who will take communion but communion won't take them, simply because they believe they are related to God on the merits of their own self-justification—by being good enough, adequate enough, believing enough and doing enough to say to God, "Now I'm worthy. Now you can love me."

Well, don't you feel it with the elder brother? Who else took care of that fatted calf? We fed it. Cleaned up after it. We watched over this whole farm and now we're expected to put on a bright face and welcome back the one who didn't even care enough to give his father his forwarding address.

It's a tragic thing to be at a celebration and not be able to celebrate. To be a wallflower at God's party and not be able to dance and sing. To miss the joy: that's to miss everything!

It's the infection of stately saints. It's the low-grade fever of religious people. It's the belief that we can actually maintain our relationship with God.

We sing, "I come to the garden alone, while the dew is still on the roses," and the Lord says, "Don't you come to my garden alone. You bring your brother with you." "But, Lord," we answer, "you don't know about my brother. He's liable to step on the roses!"

I remember three men who worked out an intricate, foolproof system of being the first people out of the sanctuary because they didn't want to talk to other people. When the Lord got hold of their lives and convinced them that caring for him meant caring for other people, and having him listen to them meant they'd have to listen to other people, a wonderful thing happened. Now they're the last people out of the coffee hour after the service because they are beginning to care about people. And now they are identified in the business community as person-centric men who are able to care for individuals, help them know the Lord, and let him deal with the problems and frustrations of life.

A strange thing happens to us as elder brothers. We think we can come to the Lord's Table and receive what God has to give us and not be concerned at all by the ache and suffering all around us. Then the younger brother comes home in a strange manner of dress with his hair not cut the way ours is and the Lord says, "Come to my party and let's celebrate together!"

What is it that happens to the people of God when the blight of sameness gets on them? When the rigors of religiosity take hold, the same old routine forms ruts in their minds, and the adventure is all over?

I met a young clergyman who was twenty-five and looked sixty-five. His face was set. He could repeat the New Testament impeccably, but there was no joy in his life. I remember after we prayed together, we got up from our knees and I taught him how to do a Scottish fling.

It was the first time he had ever let go enough to enjoy himself!

There was a point when David loved the Lord so much that there was nothing to do but dance before the Ark. I believe that's what ought to happen to the people of God when the inner experience of grace so possesses them that infectious joy radiates in their fellowship.

"Come unto me, all ye who labor and are heavy laden, and I will give you rest."

The Lord Jesus takes you by the hand and says, "Come to my Table even if you feel unworthy. Come to the party even if you think you are justified in yourself."

He breaks us all open and then melts us all together into a oneness only members of his Body can know. A fantastic love begins to spread among us—the love of his own Spirit.

Come ... let's celebrate.

The living Lord has invited us to his Table.

6

Christ Is
for the World
John 4:7-42

If you had to put five words together into the most discouraging, debilitating statement you could possibly make, what would those five words be?

If you wanted to pull the rug out from under people's enthusiasm, if you wanted to pour cold water on their eager hopes, what's the one thing more than any other you could say?

What are these five vandalizing words that confuse and hurt and deplete? I would like to suggest they are these: "It won't make any difference!"

If there's any anguish we feel at times, it is this. Regardless of what's said or done, it won't make any difference. Regardless of what happens in our lives, it won't make any difference.

We read the daily newspaper, wince at the panorama of human need, and we pray to God that somehow he'll show us the way to make a difference in our world. In the quiet of our own hearts we garrison a slender hope that if we really trusted him, asked for his direction and his strategy, we could begin to do something about it. And then a friend puts his arm around us and says, "It won't make any difference!"

Or perhaps in the midst of our own discouragement about our relationships, we dare to believe that if we really trusted Christ we could have a new love. A new attitude. A new enthusiasm. And then in that unbandaged moment the debilitating discouragement incarnated in these five words becomes our greatest enemy—"It won't make any difference!"

I believe that as we meet together around this Table, this is perhaps our greatest enemy.

There is a bottomless inner feeling that takes hold of people when they think about the world in which we live. How can you believe in a just and loving God in a world like this? A world of urban crises, of Viet Nams, of shaky détente and open hostility? Does it, we ask, make any difference what we do?

Did it make any difference that God came and lived and died and was raised up on this planet? And those of us who have dared to trust him and turn our lives over to him, the greatest thing we face is the sinister doubt that it may not have made any difference.

Quickly now I would like to suggest the five most powerful words. If you had to put together five words to make a statement. that would somehow uncap the reservation in people's minds, would give them the freedom to dare to dream again, would unleash them to hope and move with confidence and strength—what would those five words be?

I'd like to suggest they are what this whole sacrament says to us this morning. This life-infusing, enthusiasm-giving, empowering assertion for your world and mine is profoundly stated in the communion symbols before us: "Christ himself is the difference!"

Simply and directly I want to impress two things on your minds and hearts. One, Christ is for the *world.* Secondly, Christ is *for* the world. It's all a matter of emphasis, but when these two great truths are brought together they declare the meaning of the broken body and blood of our Lord.

This past week I had a very, very busy day. From early morning it was filled with challenges, crises, and opportunities. I was late for an appointment. I ran out of my office and was about to get into my car across the street when my eye caught the sign announcing this communion service. The sign now completed reads: "Christ Is for the World—Lloyd Ogilvie." That morning it was still only partially complete and it said: "Christ Is for ... Lloyd Ogilvie."

I want to tell you that was the liberation I needed at that moment in my life! And that's the truth I want to declare to you in this moment—Christ is for you!

He's not against you. "For I am sure that neither death, nor life, nor angels, nor principalities, nor things present, nor things to come ... will be able to separate us from the love of God in Christ Jesus our Lord" (Romans 8:38, 39).

Christ is for you here at the Lord's Table, and what happens to you here is for your world.

Jesus Christ met the woman by the well. He dealt decisively with her world so that she could deal creatively with her world. What happened in her inner world related directly to what she did in her outer world, because her inner self was transformed. Her outer relationships were liberated.

And that's exactly how we come to communion. Our Lord wants to do something to our personal world so that we can transform our greater world.

The "world" as a technical, biblical term means "the realm of the unredeemed." Any segment, any subculture, any elite—any realm of existence which does not know that Jesus Christ is Lord—that's the world according to the New Testament. When it says, "God so loved the world that he gave his only Son," it implies that God loved to the death in Jesus Christ all realms of existence that did not know of his power, his forgiveness, and his direction.

And so any dimension in us that is not under his lordship—he still suffers for that in this communion service. He continues the sacrifice of Calvary for that in us which is not yet touched by his forgiving power. And then through us, he moves out redemptively into our homes, our families, our offices, shops, foundries, neighborhoods.

He continues to suffer until the world and its kingdoms are claimed for him.

Note the tender way Jesus dealt with this woman. What a sensitive communicator he was! Before he gave to her, he received from her. Before he gave her concepts, he gave her a relationship. There was trust and openness and tenderness growing between them.

She was understandably astounded at first. First, that a Jew should ask a Samaritan for a drink. Secondly, that a man should ask a woman.

The rabbis used to pray in the synagogue: "O Lord, I

thank you that in your goodness you did not create me a woman." Can you imagine that? Some prayed that at no time would they have to see a woman or have to talk to her on the street. The reason many of their faces were bruised, according to one scholar, is that they walked on the streets with their eyes closed because they were afraid they might look on a woman.

I'd like to tell a few of those rabbis what they missed!

The woman was astounded that Jesus wanted to talk to her. Was he like all the rest of the men she had met? Did he want to grasp something from her without really caring about her? They began to talk.

I have a deep feeling that in a wonderful way, Christ's eyes, his countenance, and his whole being drew her in tenderness. He told her about a kind of relationship that quenched the hunger and thirst of a human being so completely that he would never thirst again. Eagerly she grasped for the gift. "Oh, give me that water that I may never thirst or have to come here again!"

But suddenly she was rubbed raw in the inner place of her being. Because Jesus knew he could not give her what she wanted until God dealt with what she needed, he said, "Go, get your husband." Her psyche ached like flesh that had been torn apart as she confessed, "I have no husband."

Having set the boundary, the direction of the relationship, Jesus began to work with her. He exposed the central problem standing between her and the power of the living God and she tried to slip away by arguing theology.

How often that's the way with all of us. Surface scars

and tissues demand first attention. It is said that conservative Christians most need to have their morals dealt with; liberals need their thinking clarified.

This woman wanted to debate Mount Gerizim's precedence over Jerusalem—the Samaritan's place of worship over the Jew's. Jesus refused to discuss either. The issue, he insisted, was that God is a Spirit, not a place. One begins to worship in truth when one is completely open to him.

You see, Jesus was the light of the world and he knew that the darkness of man's mind had to be penetrated, that the moral life of this woman had to be healed, and that every dark thing within her had to be exposed. The same thing is true for you and me.

Jesus knows about our world. Not just the sphere of our existence but the secret realms of our life. He knows the memories we hope no one can ever probe. The secret plans. The expenditures. The savings. The false gods and futile images. He knows us absolutely and utterly.

We cry out with the Psalmist, "O Lord, thou hast searched me ... and knowest when I sit down and when I rise up; thou discernest my thoughts from afar. Thou searchest out my path and my lying down, and art acquainted with all my ways. Even before a word is on my tongue, lo, O Lord, thou knowest it altogether. Thou dost beset me behind and before, thou layest thy hand upon me" (Psalm 139:1-5). There is no escape. There is no place to go.

And that is both the most awesome and the most exciting thought in the world!

Because he knows, he can heal us. As we eat the

bread and take the cup, the tender, life-giving Spirit moves among us and we are able to see those things that keep us from him. And like the liberated woman who went back to her village—not with new mind-boggling concepts of theology but with a profound life-changing experience—we, too, will leave the Lord's Supper wanting to do something about our world.

That's what it means to be a witnessing Christian. Not to know more or believe more than others, but to live so profoundly, so openly, so vulnerably that Jesus Christ gets at us where we hurt and hope. What we have to share with people is that he can make a difference. That he is the difference for life today.

Of course they all wanted to see him. Not the clairvoyant. Not the integrationist. Not the pro-feminist. They wanted to come and touch and know and experience the person who could liberate them, too.

We all want it. We all need it.

As the panorama of the needs of our world passes before us, we recognize that what *we* need, our immediate world needs. And it is into that world that we are sent believing that Christ is the difference—that things don't have to be the way they are. The reason our urban culture, our institutions, our families are the way they are is that we are the way we are. We don't believe that what happens to us here can change the world.

The issue is not whether the Lord can make a difference or not, but whether we will allow him to make his difference through us. The woman by the well did not draft a strategy of witnessing to the people in her village. She simply could not resist the impelling urge to tell her townspeople what Christ had said to her and done for her. Her mind immediately leaped to these people as the ones whom she had to tell. An authentic experience of Christ's grace always does that. We can't contain it. The people in whom Christ has made a difference, really, want to share the difference he has made in them. That's a telling test of whether he has been allowed to do his reconciling, healing work in us: that we can't wait to spread the good news. Efforts to press people into witnessing or caring about people are futile and guilt producing.

The question then is: How has Christ made a difference for us? Where does he need to make a difference in our attitudes, relationships and life-style? A way to discern that is to consider what you would ask him to do in you if you truly believed that taking communion is to have a deep conversation with him. Tell him about your most pressing hurt or hope. Ask for his healing and specific guidance. Be sure of this: he will answer as you take the broken bread and the cup.

Then, if we are willing, the very things he deals with in us will become the point of identification with others. We will have both sensitivity to listen and also concrete illustrations from our own lives. The experience of Christ's interventions in our lives produces the intensity of our excitement over what he can do in others.

But what about the complicated social problems which fester in the flesh of our nation and communities? Here around the Table we are reminded of the sacrificial love of God in the Cross and the supreme power of the resurrection. We need both if we are to become hopeful people in the difficulties of our time. The things which broke God's heart will break ours. But the same power which raised Jesus from the dead will be at work in us to guide our efforts, do the humanly impossible, and see evil overcome with good. All the power of God is released through the name of Jesus. What we need is the boldness to go into those situations the Lord has put on our agenda with the belief that the power of the resurrection will be at work enabling unanticipated wisdom and discernment, unexpected openings, and unpredictable breakthroughs we never thought were possible. The world is the way it is because Christians will not dare to care, fortified by the power of God. All things are possible for those who believe. Our families, companies, churches and complicated social evils do not have to remain as they are!

Now let's dare to be specific. We can aim at nothing and hit it. But if we ask our Lord to tell us the particular people and problems he wants each of us to confront as we leave this Table, we can know he will be with us. He will tell us what to say and how to respond. Closed doors will be opened. He will go before us to open people's minds and create a viable receptivity. When we are unsure or discouraged, he's a prayer away. "Lord, what next? What should I say or propose?" I have seen marriages liberated, families reconciled, offices changed, and impossible situations unbound. But in each case there was a person who dared to believe that Christ is the difference.

The miracle that happens at communion is that we are suddenly gripped by the realization that Christ is both for us and our world. Limitless insight, discernment, wisdom, and motivating power are available to you and me. When we allow him to get to the core of our needs the way he did with the woman by the well, we will feel differently, be different people and make a difference in this world that is longing to hear and see the truth that things don't have to be the way they are. As you pass these symbolic promises of hope to one another, encouragingly say the powerful words of communion: Christ himself is the difference!

7
Thinging It

Romans 12:9-21

A new term was unashamedly added to young adult jargon several years ago to describe a relationship between two persons who agree to be together and use each other without any continuing responsibility. It is called "thinging-it."

Both people in this synthetic relationship agree to be less than complex human beings with profound need. They disregard their personhood and are willing to fling caution and concern to the winds to willingly use each other. The ultimate good, the subsequent happiness, the real value of another person is disregarded for the enjoyment of the brief now. They simply "thing-it" together.

After the first blush of consternation over this depersonalizing practice, I got to thinking about many of the relationships of our lives. My conclusion is that "thinging-it" is not confined to the young adult subculture. It could be used to describe the way in which we live much of our life.

THE CUP OF WONDER

Martin Buber said that a true meeting with another happens when an "I-thou" relationship involving respect and adoration of the unique personhood of the other occurs. This is in contrast to the "I-it" relationship where we use the other person as an object or thing.

Now "thinging-it" goes one step further. It is an "it-it" relationship. We become willing to be a thing and to use other persons as things.

In whatever circumstance we use another person only as a means to some end, we are guilty of an "it" relationship. The needs, feelings, hopes, and dreams of the other are disregarded in our desire to gain something for ourselves or the cause in which we become involved. Personhood is either set aside or becomes secondary to the goal we have set. People become necessary for our purpose, and regardless of what happens to them, we use them as we would use material objects.

How important are material things to you? If your house were in flames and you had gotten all the people out to safety, what three things would you return and risk your life for? An heirloom? A valuable piece of art? A safety deposit box? Cancelled checks for justifying conversation with the IRS? Some icon of memory having esoteric significance for the family? What?

The question is a good one because it focuses on the things in our lives which are crucial to us. One man whose questionable humor betrayed something much deeper gave this answer: "What do you mean? There are three things I would get out of a burning house before I would worry about the people!"

Brash hyperbole? I wonder. To know this man intimately is to discover a disturbing lack of love for himself. He "things-it" with himself. The people of his life therefore are treated with the same absence of respect and dignity. His own lack of self-affirmation is expressed in niggardly negation of the people he says he loves. His need for them debilitates his love for them.

"Thinging-it" becomes a pattern of relationship in our increasingly depersonalized society. Eventually we lose our self-appreciation to the point that, inadvertently or planned, this devaluating habit becomes the conditioned response to the people around us.

All of us are vulnerable to this tendency. I believe that the family becomes the breeding ground for this psychologically congenital sickness. "Thinging-it" as a response to family life begins early. It is fertilized in its seedling growth when the child begins to feel that his success or proper behavior is necessary, not for his own welfare and maturity, but for the ego-satisfaction of his parents. As parents, often our choicest expressions of affirmation and encouragement are geared to the "ought" of expectation in a child's psyche so he will not disappoint our image. Our children must do and be something for us or we feel we have failed. I am sure the rebellion syndrome in our lives and many of our children is related to this subliminal suspicion. Eccentric, excessive behavior patterns often express our desire to be loved in spite of what we have done or are.

The friendships of life often perpetuate this "thinging-it" syndrome. We need people more than we love them. We need their approval, support, energy, talent, money, or votes to accomplish something. Early in life we learn how to say and do the things which will get them marching to the drumbeat of our will.

Marriage can easily be an extension of this. We need another person to fill our loneliness, plans, or dreams. Often our deepest expressions of love are simply, "I need you, want you, desire you ... because of what is lacking in me."

"But wait a minute," you say. "Who's any different? To honestly admit our needs and find someone to fill them is the stuff of life!" Perhaps. But what is happening to the other person while we are being fulfilled?

A friend was blankly dumbfounded when his wife, who had been presenting to the world a beautiful picture of a successful executive's wife, suddenly became negative and uncooperative. The truth is that as he races pell-mell down the road to stardom, her needs are being ignored. Suddenly he cannot understand why she approaches sex as a perfunctory responsibility and not with the delight of people in love. She has belatedly discovered that she is a thing. Because of it she is willing to relate to him as a thing and is no longer able to meet his needs.

We also "thing-it" in working relationships. We expertly mesh the skills, intelligence, and experience of people around us to produce an effective, goal-attaining team. But what happens when the human needs of a person in the machinery make him less than productive?

"Thinging-it" can take on very subtle dimensions. We can actually use the skills of sensitivity and caring to keep a person productive for our own ends. We learn how to say and do the things which will bring the right response. By the right compliment or cajoling, we keep a person in line—our line—for our goal, of course.

Even the church can become an extension of our "thinging-it" society rather than a model of a profoundly personalizing quality of life. Quite honestly, most of us go to church for what we can get out of it. We all need spiritual help and encouragement. Our presence here is an admission that we need God's love and guidance for our lives. For some, the church offers a means to power. As long as it provides something for our carefully defined expectations, we will participate in it and support it. When it doesn't, we use the power of the pledge and lack of attendance to express disapproval.

Inside these walls we often barter people's needs to get a church program established and keep it going. A willing volunteer can be ground into the ecclesiastical machinery and crushed into many molds to fit the patterns inherited by years of unexamined procedures. The church becomes something we join and participate in as long as our desires are met, rather than something we are by virtue of being God's person.

Tragically, we even "thing-it" with God.

Do we love God for what he is or for what he can do for us? Many of us trust in a God-shaped blur—an impersonal power we hope will be the intervening force to step in and do for us what we cannot do for ourselves. What he can give—not who he is—is the motive and extent of our piety.

The most amazing good news of grace is that God is willing to meet us there!

But he will not leave us there. He wants us to love him and serve him not for what he will get, but in response to what he has already given. Life takes on a

THE CUP OF WONDER

new perspective and all of our relationships are reoriented when we experience a love which is not dependent on our goodness or our performance.

God will not manipulate us!

That's the point of the story of the rich young ruler. He was attracted by the quality of life Jesus communicated and came to seek it. "What must I do?" he asked. The answer: "Go, sell all you have, and give it to the poor!"

Does this suggest that God would love him more after his sacrifice? No! It means that this young man who could always manipulate his environment with his bank account was to be stripped of that manipulative commodity. This was the only way he could discover that God loved him regardless of what he could give or do. It was too much for the young man. He could not believe that he could be loved for himself and he turned away. But note, though he could have been of inestimable help in his mission, Jesus did not run after him to manipulate him. He loved him too much for that.

Paul's description of the Christian way to love is in our text. It simply says: "Let love be without dissimulation" (KJV). Recent translations put it: "Let love be genuine" or "Love must be completely sincere." The Greek word used to describe this quality of love means true love—love that comes from a pure heart—capable of being judged under the sun. I like the old King James word for the Greek, "dissimulation." True love does not say or do the thing when another effect is intended. Dissimulated love is manipulative.

It is hard for some of us to admit that we use people

Thinging It

as things. According to Everett Shostrom,[1] there are top-dog and under-dog manipulators. Top-dog manipulators control with criticalness, aggression, measured demands, and brute strength. But the under-dog has an arsenal, too. Weaklings control with mock sensitivity. Clinging vines with dependency. The nice guy with warmth. Whatever the mode, the purpose is to get what we want when we want it from the people of our lives.

The opposite of manipulation is actualization. An actualizing person is one who appreciates himself and others as persons of unique worth and potential. Hopefully we are all somewhere in the process of becoming actualizers.

Most of us are capable of exalted moments of that kind of loving. Sustaining it in the competitive marketplace and in our often fragile relationships is the real problem. Too often we defect and resort to manipulation. We fail to allow the crisis in the relationship to become a fresh discovery of Christ's limitless, contagious love.

Our relationship with Christ and the relationships of our lives are brought into sharp and almost simultaneous focus as we come to the Lord's Table. With these symbolic emblems of bread and wine, we celebrate his death for us, his continuing life in us, and his hope for the quality of our relationships with others.

The shadow of the cross falls over our Communion Table. Two words we use so often at communion now

---

[1] *Man the Manipulator*, Everett L. Shostrom. (Nashville: Abingdon Press, 1967).

become the hope of being free of "thinging-it." Active,
dynamic words—*broken; poured out.* Christ's body was
broken for us; his blood was shed. He did not "thing-
it" with us on the Cross. He loved us to the uttermost.
No manipulation. Not a moment of dissimulation. To
know him and the love of his Cross heals the taproot of
our problems. Here finally, is one who loves us as we
are, who will not trifle with our affections. There is no
escape. Nothing we can do or say to make him affirm or
approve us. He has offered that already. Nothing we can
be that will make him stop loving us. His love won't
quit; his forgiveness is given before we ask.

Wait at the foot of the Cross long enough, until you
know that you have one solid, unchanging relationship
that is authentic and eternal. Now begin to imagine,
who needs that kind of love from me? Picture them, feel
their presence, their anxious need for your love. What
would it be like this next week to love without demand
for response, to give yourself away without reward, to
simply take people as they are, where they are. The
same words we use for the bread and wine are now the
active verbs of a new life. We are to be broken-open
bread and poured-out wine for people as persons not
things. The Lord's words echo in our hearts. "If any
man would come after me, let him deny himself, take
up his cross and follow me." We have been called to be
a new breed of lovers of people in a "thou-thou" depth
and freedom.

Jesus is faithful to his promise. If we make this opportunity to eat bread and drink wine together our confession of our "thinging-it" lives, then he will come
within us and love through us.

Thinging It

"I am the living bread which came down from heaven," Jesus said. "Except ye eat of the flesh of the Son of Man, and drink of his blood, ye have no life in you... He that eateth of my flesh and drinketh my blood, dwelleth in me and I in him" (John 6:51, 53, 56).

8
Resolution and Absolution
John 8:1-11

"Go, and sin no more!"

What an impossible admonition! Who could live up to that challenge? How could this poor woman—this plaything for men's lusts, this pawn in the hands of the Pharisees—go and sin no more?

Even if she were freed economically and emotionally from the foul practice of using her body for a brief relationship with another person, how could she go and be free from sin? Every new day would bring things to be done which would be left undone. Each persistent sunset would witness another day in an incomplete and sinful life.

After a statement like that, how could she ever face Jesus again for forgiveness? What would he say a second time? If all her instant hopes and dreams for a new life came tumbling down with some new failure and she came to him again, what would he do?

The testimony of the gospel is clear—his words would be exactly the same!

Resolution and Absolution

Out of love deep and unchanging he would affirm again the forgiveness and unconditional love of God which he came to make real to mankind. He affirms them still in the symbols of Holy Communion.

The woman could make resolutions, but only God could give absolution. We all make earnest promises to God and to ourselves. At the edge of each new year. On the threshold of new relationships. At the grave of a loved one. At the Lord's Table.

Yet again and again we are engulfed with an overpowering sense of guilt and frustration when we are forced to realize how little has been changed. How little we have affected the tense problems of our society and the deep, complicated problems of our world.

Where is the hope? Simply that we resolve and God absolves. God is here to forgive. To heal and release us by his love. Do we have the need to accept a love like that?

What does this say about our God? Will he always forgive? What does this say about his people? Will they always be doomed to a circular existence of spiritual failure, futility, and forgiveness? Where is the victorious, abundant life about which Jesus speaks?

The story of the woman taken in adultery expresses a profound truth about God and how he deals with our sin and failure. It is obvious that the Pharisees had plotted long and carefully for this confrontation. They had put together their legal and intellectual skills for the infamous purpose of discrediting and impaling Jesus on the horns of a dilemma. At this time it was not at all unusual to bring a difficult legal question to a rabbi for a decision. But this volatile question was carefully packaged for more than that. The plan was to expose Jesus and provide them with legal basis for doing away with him.

The trap was set. Jesus was being lured into it. The people and the architects of the plan stood watching with anticipation.

What an electrified triangle of human dynamics that was! Here were the Pharisees—bitter, legalistic, and cold—disguising their trap with high-sounding civic overtones, a desire to purge Jerusalem of its evil morals. Their whole attitude was one of cruelty. The heartlessness with which they blasted their victim was as immoral as her promiscuity. Her virtue was nothing to them. She was a thing to be used to challenge Jesus' popularity and ensnarl him in his own words.

They had listened long enough to his words of love and forgiveness. What of the Law? How long could he go on violating the blessed order they loved and obeyed?

Then there was the woman. Empathize, if you dare, with her. Only moments before, she had been engulfed in the false security of a stolen affection. How little we know of the circumstances which caught her in this web of deceit. What flirtation, what flattery, what promises, what longing for tenderness, what unconscious parental influence, what aching unfulfilled wells in her own psyche had broken down her own sense of the sacredness of marriage?

We do not know. Her only passion now is the anguish of shame and bitter remorse at the feet of Jesus. Added to this is the searing realization that she is being used in a diabolical plot about which she knows nothing.

Consider Jesus. His ministry to the sick and confused had been bluntly halted by this inhuman interruption. The issues were immediately clear to the Master. If he defended the Law, the multitude would feel that he no longer sympathized with the publicans and sinners. If he took issue with the scribes and Pharisees, he could be accused as a law-breaker and a defamer of the Mosaic covenant. He was pitted against Moses as well as his accusers.

He knew the Law well. Many a time he must have read Leviticus 20:10—"If a man commits adultery with the wife of his neighbor, both the adulterer and the adulteress shall be put to death." And Deuteronomy 22:11—"If a man is found lying with the wife of another man, both of them shall die ... so you shall purge the evil from Israel."

Would he be able to oppose himself and his opinions against this specific statement of the Law? By what loophole could he avoid the dilemma they had contrived?

"Teacher, this woman has been caught in adultery. Now in the Law, Moses instructed us to stone such. What do you say?" This they *said* that they might have some charge to bring against him.

The Greek verb *said* in this passage is in the imperfect tense, suggesting that they prodded him repeatedly to make him convict himself. Jesus looked into their accusing, hate-filled faces and heard them clamor for an answer. His pity for the woman and his deep concern for those who accused her ached in his heart.

Jesus bent down and wrote with his finger on the ground. The air was charged with suspense. Why did he do this and what did he write?

There have been many explanations. Some have said he wrote out of sheer embarrassment and shame at the coldheartedness of the Pharisees. Others have suggested it was to channel his anger until he could speak clearly. Another view is that he needed a moment to think over his answer to this loaded question.

None of these is adequate. I believe the clarity of the Greek and the historical data in Jerome's translation suggest something quite different. The Greek word for *write* means to write down against someone. To write against as in the Greek translation of Job 13:26, "Thou writest bitter things against me."

Did he write one word? Several accusing words? We do not know. Perhaps his finger spelled out pride, anger, hypocrisy, avarice, lust—words that set off a penetrating moral inventory. Perhaps only a single word was used, a terrifying word which exposed their inner sins and desires.

The Greek word *anomartetos* means much more than "without sin." It means without sinful desire. These men had heard Jesus' judgment on this: "You have heard that it was said, 'You shall not commit adultery,' but I say to you that everyone who looks at a woman lustfully has already committed adultery with her in his heart" (Matthew 5:27).

Here, according to William Barclay, is what Jesus was really saying. "All right, you may stone her, but only if you have never wanted to do the same thing yourselves. If you have no deep and hidden sins in your own being, then you may cast the first stone."

The dilemma was dramatically reversed. If the accusers said they had no sins, they would blaspheme God. If they said they had sinned, they would not only lose stature in the people's eyes but become liable to be stoned to death themselves. There was nothing to do but leave. The oldest left first. "One need only to grow older to become gentler in one's judgments," Goethe said. "I see no fault committed which I could not have committed myself."

Finally there was no one left but Jesus and the woman. To quote Augustine: "There remained a great misery and a great pity." He held great power over her. He could have stoned her, for he was sinless.

"Has no one condemned you?" he asked. "No one, Lord."

Heaven and earth were held in balance. What would Jesus say? Then came those fantastic words of absolution and admonition, "Neither do I condemn you; go, and do not sin again."

The soiled plaything of men encountered the perfect holiness of Jesus who loved her as she had never been loved before. Not for what she could give, but for who she was. The Pharisees had seen her as a thing to be used; Jesus saw a person. The Pharisees used her as an accessory to contrivance; Jesus respected her as a human being. The Pharisees saw only the past, "the very act." Jesus saw only the future, "Go, and sin no more." The Pharisees wanted to stone her. Jesus wanted to save her.

Jesus' major concern was for this woman. No standard of judgment, no preconceived notion, and no unresolved complex within him kept him from sensing her need to be loved, forgiven, and released to live a new life. Jesus' attitude toward her is consistent with the whole Bible's concern for persons.

This is what Paul Tournier calls the personalism of the Bible. He reminds us that God says to Moses, "I know you by name." And to Cyrus, "I am the Lord which called thee by name." God's relationship to his people was always modeled through individuals whom he loved and released to be all that he had created them to be.

Jesus saw this woman in her desperate need for love and forgiveness. How he treated her is a divine paradigm of how he will treat us if we meet his holiness with the same kind of honesty at the Lord's Table.

Our Lord's attitude toward this woman as a person contained three basic ingredients. First, it included mercy. He used his authority to love people into goodness. It was his deepest wish to express forgiveness to them so they might try a new life based on his power. He pitied this woman in her plight and yearned that she might have the acceptance which would break the undertow of sin in her life.

The second ingredient was a fantastic challenge. "Go, and sin no more." He believed that the creative power of his love for her would release her from the necessity of sinning any more. At the root of this challenge is Jesus' faith in human nature, and this is the third ingredient.

Jesus believed that the knowledge of the forgiveness and the never-ending acceptance of God is the only basis for truly creative and lasting change. The nature

of God revealed here is the nature of never-ending forgiveness. We cry out: "What kind of God is this who
can forgive again and again? Does he have no moral
fibre? No basis of judgment? No requirements of his
people?"

The Lord God of Israel demands more of his people
than any of the gods of ancient times. It is in Jesus
Christ that the power for men to fulfil God's requirements is given. It is in the knowledge that we can dare
to try to sin no more, and yet should we fall there is
forgiveness. The deepest bind under which human nature exists is the bind of self-assertive sin which makes
us unwilling to receive love. Once we are convinced
that God's love cannot and will not change, then the
compulsiveness of our sin is broken and we are released to live life as it was meant to be lived.

Arthur John Gossip put it this way: "If the mystery of
divine forgiveness toward us does not create in us a
new horror of sins to which we had grown accustomed
or which we like too well to renounce, and a new power
to resist them ... then in us God's tremendous plan of
salvation has as yet entirely failed. Even his willingness
to save us cannot save us from our doom."

But we are here. God's loving entreaty has been
heard!

This then is our hope as we come to the Table of the
Lord. The memory of the past aches within us. The
hope of the future yearns within us. Tokens of his fresh
grace are before us.

We shall make firm our resolves as we reach for the
bread and raise the cup, but it shall not be the firmness
of our promise or the diligence of our activity that will

make the permanent change within us. It will be the love of God.

That love whose absolution and forgiveness is forever prismed in the broken body and shed blood of his Son.

9

You Are a Gift
John 19:26, 27

Feel it if you will. Let it happen to you if you dare. Take the most precious of your children. Hold him in your mind's eye. Feel your love and care for him and place him upon the cross.

Take the most precious friend of your life. The person with whom you've known joy and fun and sorrow. With whom you share the deep bonds of caring. Place him upon the cross and watch him writhe in pain.

The nails driven into those beloved hands are driven into our hands. The muscles excruciatingly stretched are our muscles. The terrible burning of his tongue and mouth is in our tongue and mouth. We feel it all as if we were there ourselves because the most precious person in all the world is there on our behalf.

Feel it. Experience it if you will.

Mary had been told it would happen to her. Simeon's prophecy as he took her babe in his arms was clear and unconfused, "Behold, this child is set for the fall and the rising of many in Israel, and for a sign that is spoken against (and a sword will pierce through your own soul also)" (Luke 2:34, 35).

She felt that sword now. Piercing. Twisting. Wrenching. And if the agony of watching was not excruciating enough, painful, exacerbating memories would not let her go.

As she looked upon him her focus drifted. She re-experienced the holy moment the angel of the Lord came to her. "Blessed art thou among women." He told her that God's Son would be conceived in her as a gift of the Holy Spirit. With sweet thanksgiving she surrendered body and soul to the Holy Spirit and took in tranquility what God might bring. As she waited, she felt within her the arousal of a holy child.

The night he was born, angels declared the glory of it. "Glory to God in the highest." And they were talking about her son.

But there was always a cross over his creche. And a deep uncertainty as she watched him grow. When he became a man and went off to lead his people, she wondered what she could do to remain his mother and yet be his follower.

Again and again she faced the fact that she did not understand. It surfaced first at the marriage in Cana when he turned on her maternal request and said, "Woman, what have you to do with me?" There was a difference now in their relationship. Then when she and his brothers were separated from him by the crowd and they couldn't get through even for a moment of family closeness, they sent word to him. "Your mother and your brothers are here."

The message was simple and clear. He looked to the

sky and paused a while. Then he looked at the crowd, singling them out one by one with dramatic intensity. Only then did he answer, and his words cut deep into the heart of this one who carried love so gently—"Who is my brother and my mother ... but everyone who does the will of the Father."

She remembered the time she came to try to take him home and nurse him. "Your son is mad," they said. "Possessed with Beelzebub." She longed to surround him again with her comfort and care. But he would not.

Most difficult of all to understand was the time he said, "If anyone comes to me and does not hate his father and mother and wife and children and brothers and sisters, yes, and even his own life, he cannot be my disciple" (Luke 15:26). Then he put it squarely and clearly. "Whoever does not bear his own cross and come after me, cannot be my disciple" (verse 27).

It was then she knew. No longer was it enough to be just his mother. She too had to make a decision of faith to be his follower.

It was all over now. This precious son of her own womb was dying upon the cross.

Next to her was John, the beloved disciple, the one Jesus dared to love especially. A friend. A compatriot. A fellow participant in the great vision. John had at first been a follower of John the Baptist, but when the fore-runner pointed to Christ and said, "Behold, the Lamb of God, who takes away the sin of the world," John caught the cadence of the direction of the Master and followed him.

But John, along with his brother James, had great ambitions. He could remember the time his mother went up to Jesus and said, "When you get to glory, I want one of my sons on your right and the other on your left." How gentle Jesus was with her unabashed nepotism. He turned to her sons. "Are you able to drink the cup that I drink?" Jesus asked. John could remember the enthusiasm and vigor with which he answered, "Yes, I am able."

Now he wasn't so sure. As he looked at the cost of discipleship and saw what obedience to God had cost his Master, he wondered. And John, the one who stood beside Jesus at the time of the celebration of the first communion, stood close to him now. Later as John the Apostle, he wrote his Gospel, encouraging letters to the early church, and the message of the triumphant adequacy of Christ in Revelation.

There is a third person who is often missed at the foot of the cross. Her name is Salome. According to the records, she was John's mother by natural birth. Do you catch the significance? It was Salome who demanded a seat at the right hand for her son John.

Salome was the sister of Mary. Isn't it a tender thought that this same John who wrote the Gospel didn't add a little parenthesis after he referred to her as "the sister of Mary"—("that's my mother"). Instead he wrote his historical account of the life of Jesus with only a few brief personal references.

But now, allow your mind's imagination to grip that scene again in the light of these essential relationships. Jesus has just said to John, "Son, behold your mother," and it was clear he was not indicating Salome. It was his own mother. To Mary, Jesus said, "Woman, behold your son," not signifying himself but pointing away from himself to his beloved disciple.

The true nature of the church was expressed there at the foot of the Cross. Not just at Pentecost. It was infused at Pentecost. The church was experienced when the crucified Christ, suffering for sins, gave these two people whom he loved with the love of eternity to each other.

And that's what it means to take communion!

It means to witness the tokens of his torn body and poured-out blood and know that he did it for me. For each of us. We are forgiven. Accepted. Set free. Empowered to live a new life filled with love and grace.

But it also means that in this same moment he points you to someone else. Someone beside you or near you now. Someone in your family. Your neighborhood. At your job. He says, "Behold your brother, your mother, your father, your sister," in a sense that lifts us out of the isolation of a single family and lifts us into the liberation of the family of God.

To take communion, to receive communion, means that Jesus Christ gives us a gift to each other. The bonds of love are strengthened as never before. It is only when we recognize this that we grasp the essential nature of the church.

There has never been a time in history when more church buildings dotted the landscape. Never a time when more has been written about the nature of the church. And I believe that never in history has the experience of the church been so difficult to discover and extend.

It is for this reason I believe that what God has called us to at his Table is so awesome and wonderful. It means that as we pass the bread and the cup, giving the signs of the covenant to each other, no one can sit separated from the others. Symbolized in the broken bread and the cup of the new covenant are his suffering and death, his caring for each one of us—and that's precisely what we are meant for with each other.

We belong to each other. We were called together and given to each other. The hopes and dreams, the aches and fears of one, concern everyone.

As we pass the bread and wine, we offer ourselves with these simple words, "Here I am. Called, redeemed, healed, and set apart to be God's gift to you. And as God will not stop loving me, I cannot stop loving you. As God forgave me, I now forgive you. As God accepts me, I now accept you."

An electric charge goes through the sanctuary as the great miracle of all time is reenacted. What God intended in creation is now fulfilled as a body of believers from different occupations, different backgrounds, and with different degrees of training and need are suddenly galvanized together with the power of his love.

The church is alive. Right here. In our midst.

Woman, behold that son next to you. Brother, take hold of your brother. Sister, that person beside you is God's gift to you. Every father among you, your children are here, for we are the people of God.

Behold your mother. Behold your son.

Amen.

10
Prayer and Our Worries
Matthew 6:24-34

One of my greatest memories is a trip my eldest son and I took through Scotland. We have as a common hobby Scottish lore and history. And the love of the bagpipe.

Some good friends of ours had arranged for us to stay in a Scottish castle. The laird showed us through all of the rooms, and we went down all of the memory-laden corridors. He told us about the furniture on which this great dignitary and that great personage of history had been seated. We saw the wonder of the gardens and later we walked along the parapets and looked out over the beautiful highlands.

This was one of the most delightful moments in the trip, simply because we not only saw the sumptuousness of this castle, but we were able actually to sleep in the bedroom of the laird of the castle.

That night when we went to bed, we got down underneath all the heavy covers, for it was cold even in the middle of summer. I can still remember looking over to my son's bed with his excited face protruding out of the covers. He said, "Hey, you know, if you had all this, it would sure be hard to die."

What are the things that make it difficult for us to die?

I believe they are our unfulfilled hopes and dreams. The outer accoutrements of our achievements. The people and possessions of our lives.

Indeed, the very things that would make it very difficult for any one of us to die today are precisely the things that make us worry. What is the circumstance or person to which your mind would dart immediately if I said today was the day of your death?

Someone once said that worry is a cycle of ineffective thought and emotion whirling around a thick center of fear. I like that description. Another definition of worry is that it is tedious molehill climbing. There are a lot of people who never get to the mountains because they are so busy working over the molehills of all the things that may happen but usually never do.

Isn't it amazing, we have fifty, sometimes sixty, perhaps seventy or at the most eighty years of life here to prepare to live forever. And yet, during these wonderful moments, most of us are stretched out on the rack of worry.

Because of it, we don't really enjoy the days of our life. We don't really live each moment as if it were the last. Each day as if it were the only one left. Each week as if this was God's gigantic gift for us to experience ... enjoy ... take delight in.

Worry is that insecure fill that we push down into the caverns excavated by our false expectations. It cannot take the burden of a bridge between where we are and where we long to be. It's marshy and unstable. It doesn't last. Worst of all, it doesn't help us when we need it most.

This surrogate fill is made up of what we know we should be and aren't. What we want to achieve but can't. What has been that we wish weren't. All that we want people to be that they can't achieve. And these are the worries we press in upon our psyches. We ruminate about them. We spend our days worrying our energies away.

A doctor did a study of his patients. For a whole year he tabulated the things that were troubling the people who came before him. Because he had a family practice, he listened to a wide gamut of human concern.

And here is the result of that study. Forty percent of the worries that had been told to him never happened. Thirty percent were related to wish dreams that people had for those around them, simply because they couldn't trust those people to God. Twelve percent of the worries were related to physical difficulties which had been caused and intensified by worry. Ten percent of the things worried about happened in the normal working out of everyday life and were impossible to control no matter what one did. And the last eight percent were valid problems that needed the attention of his skill in medicine. But all the rest of the worries were the cause of most of the distress that confronted him every day.

Amazing!

And as I listen to all of us and try to understand our lives, I find that so many of us are living at about half speed because we dare not trust God with our worries.

In his words on the Mount of Beatitude Jesus Christ dealt with this horrendous problem—the interrelationship between our worries and the power of prayer. He introduced the subject with this topic sentence: "No man can serve two masters."

That in itself is a vivid and loaded illustration when you realize that some people in his audience may have been expected to do just that. Slaves who belonged to a landowner who was captured along with his lands became the possession of the conqueror. One translation of the word slave is "a living tool." Often after an invasion the slave didn't know to whom he truly belonged—whose tool he really was.

Jesus is simply stating that you can't serve two masters at the same time. His implication is that you must serve one. He is pinpointing an existential dilemma—all of us are under ultimate allegiance to something or someone that either saps us of meaning or gives our life power.

And which of the two is it for you as you come to the Lord's Table?

What is the prevailing ethos of your life: fear, or faith? Jesus establishes the fact that life is a gift of God. A gift to be enjoyed to his glory during this brief earth life. Not a sinister obstacle course to be worried through to its conclusion.

And now Jesus used humor to drive home his point. He pointed to the birds of the air. Twittering. Flittering. Picking up their food by the provision of God Almighty. Our Lord was not advocating they should no longer work, for who is busier than a sparrow? He was commending work but with this awareness—it is the Author of Life who ultimately provides food. We need to be reminded often that the food that will sustain us next year still waits in the seed, the soil, and the rain. In the providence of God.

And then he gives a second illustration. He calls for a volunteer to step out of the crowd and add a cubit to his height by thought control. A cubit was commonly known to be eighteen inches long, the length of a forearm. Now if you can't catch the humor of that—try and stretch your body eighteen inches longer. Would you like to try? Jesus is simply saying, "You can't make yourself eighteen inches taller or stretch your life any longer, so learn to live happily inside those parameters. Use what you have and enjoy it. Then you can receive my power beyond your limited possibilities and potential."

There was a third vignette—the tiny flowers of the field. Not the gigantic, luxurious lilies but the tiny flowers that invaded the countryside, projecting their beautiful substance between weeds and rocks and eventually cloaking the whole countryside with soft purple. Now the thing about these exquisite little flowers Jesus wanted them to understand is that they lived only one day. And here's the point—if God gives life and beauty to a flower like that for only one day, isn't he more concerned for you and me who are designed in his image and destined to live forever?

And now the master teacher moves to his concluding sentence. He suggests that the only way to be liberated from worry is to seek first the kingdom of God. To be liberated from care by an ultimate care. To be free from anxiety because you are anxious about the ultimate thing.

And then, once we've been set free to care more about whether we are in the kingdom than whether we have achieved all the little time-bound things we worry about, then we are free to live one day at a time!

The worries and concerns of any particular day are quite enough. Don't press yesterday's worries into today's hours. Don't take from tomorrow into today. Today is enough to deal with in and of itself.

Do you see what Jesus has been doing to us? He has been moving us away from all the things and people and situations that make us worry, and now he is right down to that inner core of fear around which these ineffective and debilitating thoughts whirl. He wants to deal with that now. That's where communion begins, and that's where it starts its power.

There in the core of us—because he has never dealt with our ultimate allegiance, because we've never seen that we are pretending a terrible ambivalence—a terrible kind of dichotomy of allegiances exists. It exists between what we want and what he wants. Between the demands of other people and the expectations of God. It is because this terrible civil war is going on inside us that all of these things are pulled into the vortex of addictive, enervating worry.

We worry about people and what they are going to do because they have become our master—even our god. Our jobs, promotions, and demotions become inordinately important to the point of gripping despair because there is not an honest center of calm where God's Spirit dwells in the center of our being.

Prayer and Our Worries

Nor do we really believe we are alive forever. It's rather absurd when you think of how little time we allow in this span of life to get ready to live forever. If that's true then everything else—the fears, the uncertainties, the anguish—should be in perspective. All of these must be seen in the light of the fact that nothing can separate us from the love of God. Neither things present nor things to come, angels or principalities, height nor depth nor any other creature in all creation!

And it is here, as we break this bread and drink of this cup that we tangibly experience the central truth of life—he was broken for us that our hearts might not be splintered by the fragmentation of a multiplicity of loyalties. As we become whole through his brokenness, everything in our life begins to revolve around the central loyalty to him and his kingdom. Worry is replaced by what the poet called "the deep mysterious joy of absolute subjection"—to him rather than to the things and persons of our lives.

And the cup of the new covenant—the very word indicates that there now is a new relationship. That's what covenant means. The old covenant was by religion and law. The new covenant is by grace. When we drink of that cup, we know that we may go to him on the basis of his love and not on the basis of our adequacy.

And that's what heals the power of fear around which worry revolves.

Tahler, a German mystic, tells of his encounter with a beggar. He said to him, "Good-day, my friend." And the beggar said, "I've never had a bad day." "Well, a fine life to you," Tahler said. "My life has been very fine," the beggar answered. "When it rains, I praise God, and when it's sunny I praise God. When I have food I praise God, and when I'm hungry I praise God. I praise God in all things." "You speak like a king," Tahler said. "Where is your kingdom?" The beggar answered, "In my heart."

And that's where Jesus Christ said the essential issue of the quality of life is decided.

Bishop Quail was walking back and forth in his bedroom, worried and anguishing over problems he could not solve. As he retraced his footsteps again and again, his brow became knitted and he sweat with the anguish of what he was going through. In the middle of it all, he heard a voice saying to him, "Quail, you go to bed. I'll take those worries while you sleep."

That's what the invitation to communion is. As we take the cup and commune with each other, let the Lord take the worries and wrap his tender peace around you. Receive that new center of security in him.

This inner calm, this God-tooled armature of the soul will not allow ineffective thoughts to revolve around it. It will draw them all in and heal and release them.

Even so, come.

11
The Hard Saying
John 6:53-61

Many sayings of Christ are difficult. Here is one that may strike you as revolting, even ghoulish, until you catch its inner truth.

"Unless you eat the flesh of the Son of Man and drink his blood, you have no life in you."

"A hard saying" the disciples called it. "Who can bear it?" They called it hard, not nauseating, because they understood the gutsy Aramaic idiom which unlocked the thrust of Christ's challenge. When Semitic people have worked to the point of exhaustion, they say, "I have eaten my body and drunk my blood."

Does that assault your aesthetic sense? Hold on a moment. Before we judge Jesus' words as crude, note the everyday expressions of our lives when we use words like *flesh, blood,* and *heart* out of context.

We call miserly people "bloodsuckers." We say that we have sweat blood. When a demand is too difficult we exclaim: "What do you want, my life's blood?" We challenge a person to envy with the most carnivorous expression of all, "Eat your heart out, man!"

Christ chose his metaphor to dramatize the importance of dwelling in constant union with him. The allegory of the vine, "We abide in him and he in us," declares the same truth. This mystical union with Christ is not subject to the change and chance of our mortality. "Because I live, ye shall live also."

To receive from Christ what he has to give us, to have experience of his saving power, we must feed on him. There is simply no other word that expresses it with equal accuracy.

We must absorb his teaching. His character. His life. His ways. We must appropriate the virtue in him till his mind becomes our mind and his ways become our ways. Till we think as he would if he were in our situation. Until we can do what without him we could not be and do.

All this because his power has passed into us. It has become our power—no transitory thing but a permanent help.

The context of this difficult saying is also profound. Jesus had fed the multitudes bread. They followed him seeking the bread of life. He declared himself to be the Bread of Life.

To Eastern people, bread was sacred. It was the staff of life. The essential life substance. To break bread with another was a sacramental act, as significant as passing the peace pipe was to the American Indian.

To eat bread with an enemy was the sign of reconciliation. When a refugee was given asylum and broke bread in a house, his host was responsible to defend his guest even to the cost of his life.

The Hard Saying

Bread was a sacred symbol of a covenant of trust and mutual responsibility between people. When Jesus spoke of himself as the Bread of Life, he meant that he, his message, and his forthcoming sacrifice would do exactly what bread did. It would give life. Sustain life. And reconcile life.

Now put those two vital, idiomatic ideas together and you have a powerful statement. Christ is unveiling the offer of a totally new relationship with himself and a new sustenance to support it. To partake of the Bread of Life with the dedication of real participation in his life is what he offered. More than imitation. That's done of someone who's separate from us. The Christian life is not imitation, but participation with Christ living in us.

And that's exactly what this difficult word and its context mean to us as we approach the Communion Table. The bread and wine, symbols of the broken body and shed blood of Christ, are offered to us. We do not eat of his flesh literally, but we take into ourselves his spiritual personality by faith. We take his essential life, his will and purpose, into ourselves. Our breaking of bread is his pledge of power to us and our mutual love to each other.

Obedience is the key word. To eat his flesh and drink his blood means becoming involved with him as a flesh-and-blood extension of his incarnation. His hard saying becomes life-affirming. We receive his actual Spirit. In return, we give our flesh and blood.

Could it be that the reason many people turned away at this saying was not that they misunderstood it, but that they understood it too well?

They saw what Jesus' ministry cost him—loss of privacy, demands of people, misunderstanding. They sensed the gathering clouds and felt the first earth tremor of Calvary. They wanted his words and his healing, but were frightened about involvement in an unpopular cause. They were suddenly invited from observation to participation, and they recoiled in irresponsibility.

Christ did not mock the integrity of his listeners by toning down the faith. He refused to make it easier by emasculating it. Overnight the ranks thinned. Wide gaps appeared in the crowds of previously rapt listeners. His enemies relaxed a little.

Are we really any different?

We want Jesus Christ for what he can do for our peace and happiness, but we balk when the cost is a high level of involvement in doing what he did. And Jesus turns and says to us precisely what he said to his disciples, "Will you, too, turn away?"

And some of us answer: "Lord, to whom...? You have the words of eternal life!"

Archbishop William Temple said that without the experience of communion, the faith would become too vague. Too theoretical. Communion is the Word of God illustrated. It is visualized and directed to more than one of the senses in order that we might not merely hear the message of divine grace but also see and taste it. We eat and drink, which means we receive that by which we live. Just as wheat bread is the nourishment of the body, Christ is the bread of the soul.

Here's the razor edge that cuts through to the basic challenge. We are brought again to the realization of what it cost God to redeem us. No aggressive self-justification of the kind expressed in this pious verse will do at the Lord's table:

> I fight alone and win or sink,
> I need no one to make me free;
> I want no Jesus Christ to think
> That he could ever die for me.

For those of us who know our need, the words of this hard saying are like the announcement of the arrival of food to the starving.

"I am the bread of life. My flesh is food indeed, and my blood is drink indeed. This is my body. This is my blood." "It is I, have no fear." "Come to me, and I will give you rest." "I will make my home in you."

Paul sums it all up with one omega point of triumph: "Christ in you, the hope of glory!" "For me to live is Christ." "I can do all things through Christ who strengthens me."

When we partake of Holy Communion, we partake of the Spirit, the Person, the personality of Christ. His Spirit can and will enter us. And our response? To give our own body and blood—our real selves and resources—to him to be poured out in the lives of others. To be poured into the wounds of our world.

Jesus' promise is not a hard saying after all. It is a gracious promise. He offers himself to us and calls us an exciting part in his strategy to save the world. He is simply saying, "There's no communion without me and involvement in what I am doing in the world." Who would want to come to the Table without receiving either? The Savior offers to actually live in our minds, hearts, emotions and wills. Every fibre of our nature. We will never receive a better offer than that!

12
Conditions to Communion

1 John 1:5-10;
2 Corinthians 6:11-13

One week ago a very presumptuous announcement appeared in our church bulletin. It declared that Holy Communion would be held. How could we be so sure?

A banner across the main street of a little Midwest town boldly announced: "Revival meetings here next week!" What assurance did they have that scheduled meetings would bring about true revival?

What right do we have to say that because we will take communion today we will experience communion?

Did you ever consider the names used for the sacrament and the verbs employed to implement them? We speak of *observing* the Lord's Supper. *Celebrating* the Eucharist. *Receiving* the sacrament or *serving* the elements. When we use the word communion, we say we *take* it or *receive* it.

What do we mean?

The word *communion* means fellowship. It comes from the Greek word *koinonia*. Now you can do many things to fellowship, but you can't take it or serve it.

THE CUP OF WONDER

You can only experience it.

Fellowship means relationship. Christ offers himself to us for a person-to-person relationship of love, forgiveness, renewal, joy and power. We are then able to relate to one another with genuineness, freedom, and naturalness. Released from all pretense.

Holy Communion must always mean relationship with Christ and with one another. If there is separation or hostility between Christ and us—or between others and us—there can be no true fellowship. The fact that we eat a piece of bread and drink of the cup does not assure that we will have fellowship. It means that we *may* have fellowship.

The word *sacrament* stands for a visible sign of a deep, invisible bond. The elements of the service are an outward sign of this fellowship. The danger is that many of us observe the outward sign without experiencing the inner bond of fellowship with Christ himself, and there is no communion.

But this is not easy. There are conditions to that kind of fellowship. That sounds like a contradiction! How can there be conditions to relationship with Christ when the gospel assures us that his unconditional love is offered without reservation?

Both John and Paul agree that continuing fellowship with Christ and with one another must be based on absolute honesty, on our willingness to see things as they really are. This is the essential condition to communion.

For John, this fellowship waits in the word "if"—"If we walk in the light, as he is in the light, we have fellowship with one another" (1 John 1:7). Paul uses some very potent words to describe the actualization of this condition to fellowship. He writes: "Oh, our dear friends in Corinth, we are hiding nothing from you, and our hearts are absolutely open to you. Any stiffness between us must be on your side, for we assure you there is none on ours. Do reward me ... with the same complete candor" (2 Corinthians 6:11-13, Phillips).

If we practice this quality of relating, there will be confession and then communion—not only in symbol but in fact.

Let's look at our texts more deeply. John has much to say about light. For him, it is inseparable from truth. Jesus said he was both: "I am the light"; "I am the truth." Because he was the truth about God and man, he was light to man about God and about man himself. Truth is what a reality is, in and of itself. We use these symbolic words interchangeably. We say, "Yes, I see," when we mean "Yes, I understand."

When we walk in the light as Christ makes it light, we see ourselves, others, and life as they really are. Free from illusionary distortions of ignorance, pretense, and defensiveness. This is at once both the most frightening and the most releasing experience of life.

I spoke to an alcoholic about her reasons for excessive drink. "The world is so dirty," she said. "People are so mean and petty. Things as they really are seem so bleak and hopeless. I'm so inadequate to give love and bring joy. When I drink, my depression goes away."

We smile sympathetically, but what do we do to cover up reality? We get busy. We pretend. We surround ourselves with beautiful things. We paint wish images of the people in our lives and proceed to relate to them as if the images were true.

You could hardly call that walking in the light. To walk in the light is to see and tell the truth about ourselves. Robert Law put it this way: "All things must assume a different aspect in the light of God, but nothing looks so different as we ourselves do."

When was the last time you took a good look?

As physical light makes objects visible in their real character, so Christ's nature is such that he exposes everything in the moral and spiritual order in its true essence. The light of Christ forces us to see ourselves compared with his absolute moral purity. He is not an impossible standard; he is an undeniable challenge. We are meant to live and love, give and forgive, care and dare as he did!

Unfortunately there is a basic duality in all of us. The outer self is known and observed by others. The inner self which is the source of motivation, attitude, action, and reaction is known only to ourselves. The Psalmist acknowledged this when he prayed: "Behold, thou desirest truth in the inward being" (Psalm 51:6). Moral truth, he is saying, must penetrate the inner depths. There, where no one else can see, God's light exposes our personality as it really is.

Christ tells us that the eye is the lamp of the body. So long as it is undiseased and unimpaired, we can see physically. He spoke also of an inner eye which perceives truth spiritually. Now when this inner organ of perception and illumination is sick, we can no longer "see" reality. Dark places appear in our minds, our character, and our life.

A vital encounter with Christ, the light of the world,

enables us to see things as they are: God's intention for our life, and what we have done with the gift of life. The deeper our relationship goes in Christ the more we realize our need for forgiveness and his power to guide our efforts to be different.

Pride, self-will, fear of exposure, and self-sufficiency all contribute to our spiritual glaucoma. Our love for others is chilled. Dark places appear in our character and our understanding. Our judgment is faulty. Our conscience and our conduct are confused.

A great deal can be learned about the eye as well as the physical and psychological health of a person with an opthalmoscope. We need a spiritual opthalmoscope of condensing mirrors and myriad lenses to see into our inner eye. There, opaquely obstructing vision, we detect the cataracts of unconfessed sin and shortcomings which hinder our vision. We need to discover the weakness of our inner eyes, causing what Coventry Patmore called "repeated partial denials of things they have seen."

We can not bear to see ourselves as we are without exercising another of the Master's great gifts: confession. When we confess, the problem is exposed and healing can take place. Seeing spiritual problems as they are must always be coupled with confession or we will end up in hopeless depression about ourselves and others.

Walking in the light also means seeing others as they are. When Jesus restored the physical sight of the blind man, the first phase of healing took place when he saw men as trees walking. Things and people were alike.

THE CUP OF WONDER

Then Jesus completed the healing and he saw people as they were.

I believe most of us have very poor vision when it comes to seeing others. Our vision is clouded by our own desires for these persons often based on our own needs so that we cannot see them as they are. We deny others their basic right as persons to be themselves, free from possessive pressure to perform and produce.

Have you looked long and hard with penetrating perception at the people in your life? How well do you see them? Look at them honestly. Are they free and fulfilled? Even now Christ may be healing that focus and repairing that distortion. What do you see?

Paul gives us an idea of what can happen when we see ourselves and others as they are. Because his inner eye had been healed of blind spots he could say, "We are hiding nothing. Our hearts are absolutely open. We feel no stiffness. We long for complete candor." Paul had learned the condition to communion, true fellowship. He had had a breakthrough to reality in his relationships which had previously been filled with suspicion and pretense.

Note the liberating progression of these elements of fellowship. The first ingredient is that we hide nothing. What a release! The duality of thinking one thing and saying another is past, confessed and forgiven. No need to hide! The attitudes and opinions held against or about others are out in the open.

This makes possible an open heart. The heart is the seat of feeling. The openness of heart Paul described meant that these people were ready to freely feel and receive emotional warmth. How starved we all are for love and assurance! When we stop hiding ourselves or our feelings, our emotional bind is broken and we can live with abandon.

Life is feeling. We feel the love of Christ for us. Christ's love burns within us and warmth flows out from our open hearts to a cautious, cold world outside. Pretentious rigidity is gone! Judgmental aloofness which waits for love and approval before giving itself is gone! When we are stiff and not at ease with certain people, we feel we must say or do something to gain approval. The result is unnaturalness and inauthenticity. Our true self is distorted and people do not know us as we really are. There can be no love and certainly no fellowship.

But most of all, life in the light means complete candor. When we walk in light, we also talk in the light. No more slick, solicitous conversation. We can speak the truth in love to each other.

Imagine what it would be like to be free to be your true self without the necessity of pretending or projecting an image. What if you knew that the real you under the layers of assumed personality were loved and accepted? Wouldn't it be liberating to clear away all the veneer and base your whole life and all its relationships on absolute truth and honesty? Now consider what it would be to rebuild your life on that solid reality. Feel the freshness and freedom of that! Sense the delight of never having to hide again, of always being in touch with the authentic person inside without having to be defensive or protective. Life as our Lord meant it to be begins when the real person inside experiences his acceptance and affirmation. We can face anything or anyone in that light. We need never live in the shadowy corridors of duality again. Will the real you stand up? Can we say to the world, "What you see is what you get—the true me."

Would you like to meet Christ this very day? Would you like truly to know and love those around you? Would you like to experience communion as true fellowship?

Will you look at Christ as he really is? Will you see yourself as you are, in the light, without pretense? Will you dare to see others as they are, without projection? Will you see reality at it exists, without reservation?

If you will, then you can experience communion in all of its wonder and joy. The elements of bread and wine will be truly an outward sign of the deep and inner bond we have with Christ and with each other.

13
Newness Is Nowness

Lamentations 3:22, 23;
Ezekiel 11:19; Matthew 26:29;
2 Corinthians 5:17; Revelation 21:5

I want to introduce you to a very dear friend of mine. Her name is Susie.

Her story really begins with what happened to her parents, her family, and her church. And then what happened in the deepest recesses of her own heart.

Susie's parents, traditional Christians in a Presbyterian church in Bethlehem, Pennsylvania, came to a discovery which changed their lives. Some Christians who had come alive in an intensely personal encounter with Jesus Christ and his power to deal with their needs infected them with the contagion of what the Christian faith ought to be.

Instead of churchmanship they came to life. Instead of traditionalism they came to newness. Instead of the familiar, Susie's parents discovered the freshness of God in every new day. They began to share their faith with their children, and soon their family was knit together around a common commitment to Jesus Christ.

Susie was a brilliant girl. She had deep intellectual

capacities and a keen sensitivity to the power of Jesus Christ. I remember the time she knelt and I put my hand on her very alive and winsome head and blessed her in the faith. With joy she took on the ministry of Jesus Christ.

Because of her brilliant academic record, Susie was one of the first girl students admitted to Yale University. Her major was mathematics and she became a leader in her class. I recall going to a special rally Susie organized at Yale. Department heads, people who were troubled, people who had questions—she got them all together and we talked about the power of Jesus Christ as the basis of authentic intellectual growth.

We had a great time together, but at the heart of the action was this viable, dynamic young woman whose winsome love for Jesus Christ fairly sparkled around her. She would toss her head and laugh exuberantly at the sheer wonder of Christ. She was a great friend.

When Susie graduated, she was offered a choice of many different positions because of her high development in the field of mathematics. She opted instead to become part of God's strategy in reaching college students and joined the staff of Inter-Varsity Christian Fellowship.

The week before Christmas, Susie came home for her sister's wedding. At the close of the service, she stood next to the pastor and spoke the beautiful words of benediction on her sister's happiness. People said there was a particular radiance about her that day. One woman said she looked like an angel.

A few hours later Susie was on her way to Urbana, Illinois, for the Inter-Varsity Missions Conference which attracts a young breed of Christians who dare to believe they can change their world. She boarded a minibus at the airport, and as it sped along the highway, it was forced off the road by a speeding car. On impact the minibus flew into the air, its windows broke open, and the young occupants were thrown out. The bus landed on Susie's beautiful body and she died.

After talking to her mother and father, my wife, Mary Jane, and I prayed through most of the night. A great gorge wrenched open inside me. I ached to weep, but the tears would not come. Somehow the professional in me, poised to reach out to others in such hours, took over and I comforted my daughter, whose close friend Susie had always been. We asked the question, "God, why do you let things like this happen?"

When the first waves of grief had subsided enough for words, Susie's father asked me on the telephone, "Lloyd, how can we possibly celebrate the great life that lived in Susie?"

I believe the answer to that question is somehow linked with what brings us to the Lord's Table. In some twenty years of life, Susie found what some people never find in eighty or ninety years. In the rich quality of her life she superseded the bland quantity most others experience. For Susie, the new life in Jesus Christ was a profound nowness. To live vulnerably and authentically in Christ as a new creature is to live in every exquisite moment as if it were your last.

Newness is nowness!

That's what I want to celebrate with you at the Lord's Supper. Everything that Jesus Christ lived and died for is available to us right now. This became true for us at the precise moment of his intervention in our lives—when he called us to be his own person.

Because of that, we can take communion, forget the year that's past, and look to the year that's to come, knowing that God has a plan and a direction for us that neither life nor death, angels nor principalities, things present nor things to come can ever separate us from. Do you believe that?

I believe it with all my heart.

Consider this first of all—it is the essential nature of the gospel that is the source of our newness.

From the caves of Patmos, John gazed out across the Aegean Sea and pictured in his mind what was happening to the followers of Christ. He knew of their suffering. The despair that stalked their days. The bleak uncertainty that was theirs for the future. But then his darkness was flooded with a vision of the new beginning God would give to his people. I believe that John caught the exciting quality of life that is available to us right now!

"I saw a new heaven and a new earth" (Revelation 21:1).

Where is it? It's in you and me. In our relationships with each other. It is mirrored and actualized in the fresh, new beginning that God gives to us with this promise, "Behold, I make all things new" (verse 5).

There are four incredibly beautiful assurances giftwrapped for you in John's words, waiting to be realized in the newness of nowness. There will still be tears, but God himself will wipe them away. Have you ever been held in the arms of somebody who loves you and had your tears wiped away? Is there any more profound experience of the love of God than that?

There will be crying, but God will be with us in the midst of it. Incarnate in the touch of a friend or the smile of a stranger. There will be death but there will be no mourning. Do you catch the difference? We shall come to the end of our physical existence—some young and some old—but far from being a melancholy postlude to life, death is a magnificent prelude to another chapter of our eternal nowness. This life is but a fraction of eternity. Praise God for that!

And now for the bottom line—the most profound potential of all. An intimate, one-to-one relationship of filial tenderness with the Father is your present privilege. He suggests this very clearly, "I will be their God and they will be my children. I will be his father and he shall be my son."

And John continues: "To him who is thirsty, let him come and drink from the river of life." I believe that every need, every recurring thirst in our lives is satisfied by the inflowing of the Spirit of God. This too is available right now and not reserved for some future state, because newness is the character of the presence of Christ changing us right in this very moment.

The Apostle Paul experienced this newness and shared it with others. "The old has passed away, behold, the new has come. All this is from God" (2 Corinthians 5:17). He didn't have to wait for his physical death to model this new quality of life, and neither do we.

Last week I lost the key to my automobile. Four hours and a pile of locksmith's keys later I was still stranded because the girl who kept the record of the secret number from which a new key could be made had been one digit off. Finally after a desperate search of the records, the correct secret number was found and the error was discovered. When the locksmith inserted the newly made key, the ignition turned on as swiftly and sweetly as greased lightning.

Now in very practical terms it seems to me that a lot of us try to start a new year with a faulty key made from the wrong serial number. We aren't going to get off to the right beginning because we have a key that looks like the right key but can't open the new year. I believe the newness we have been considering is the key God gives us. Not something we achieve. No painstaking facsimile will do.

As Paul said in Colossians, "He has delivered us from the dominion of darkness and transferred us to the kingdom of his beloved Son" (1:13). What does he mean? He is saying that everything that was promised there in those last verses of Revelation is now available to those who enter into the esoteric realm of the kingdom of God.

A new beginning. The satisfaction of our needs. The freshness of God's power. The destruction of the power of death. The comfort of the wiping away of our tears. All of this is ours because through the reality of this feast, he takes us from the dominion of darkness and he gives us to the dominion of light—to the kingdom of God!

Ezekiel saw it, too. He saw in a vision the very Spirit of God coming into the hearts of men and in a kind of open-heart surgery, he witnessed stone-like hearts being replaced with hearts of flesh. Warm and pulsating hearts capable of receiving and becoming co-lovers with God. "I will give you one heart capable of thinking about God. And I will give you a new Spirit capable of knowing me and loving me."

With the last Scripture we feel that we have come full circle. Jeremiah quotes God as saying, "The steadfast love of the Lord never ceases, his mercies never come to an end; they are new every morning; great is thy faithfulness" ((Lamentations 3:22-23). And so the blessing God has to give comes fresh and new with each new dawn.

I believe Susie is alive at this moment as she was never alive here. I wonder about you. Are you alive in such a way that death could never hurt you? Alive in a way that life is exciting, dynamic and free?

As we come to the Table, I do not wish you a "Happy New Year." Happiness is always conditioned by circumstances and successful surroundings. Life is seldom that consistent. Joy is the quality of Christ's life in us. It is limitless and artesian, independent of transitory happiness. Jesus said, "These things I have spoken to you that my joy may be in you, and that your joy may be full" (John 15:11, RSV). His prayer to the Father was, that they may have joy fulfilled in themselves (John 17:13, RSV). Paul helped us to see the basis of this joy in Romans 14:17. "The kingdom of God does not mean food and drink, but righteousness, peace, and joy." Note the progression! Joy is the ecstasy of assurance in the soul that has experienced the peace of a right relationship with God through his grace.

A truly Christ-centered greeting for a new year is inseparably related to an ancient practice from the early church. As the saints of God would gather to break bread and share the cup, they would give the peace saying, "The peace of the Lord Jesus be with you." Peace, the source of joy. Through the peace of Christ we can have a joyous new year, regardless of what happens to us or around us. Susie knew that peace. She therefore had a joy which not even death could diminish. That's what I long for all of us to know—a newness which is now!

As we pass the bread of a new life and the cup of wonder assuring us of righteousness and peace, let us offer one another the basis of a new year, "The peace of the Lord Jesus be with you," and the hope of a new year, "Joyous new year to you!"

14
The Victory of a Deathless Life

John 11:25, 26;
1 Corinthians 15:19-22, 51-58

The death call came late at night. As I dressed and drove through the darkness, I gathered my thoughts about the reality of eternal life and the victory over death I felt sure this man who had been deeply committed to Christ had experienced.

My friend had begun a deathless life years before.

I was surprised at the number of friends who had gathered. The man who met me at the door took my coat, and with an assumed air of intimacy whispered an esoteric instruction, "We're trying to keep Jane's mind off Bob. Just keep her talking about other things."

When I got through the crowd, I found Jane seated with a group of friends trying gallantly to make small talk. It was obvious her grief was about to surge to the surface and that she needed to talk freely about Bob, his death, and the resources of hope she had for a time like this.

I asked the friends to take the party into another room. When we were alone, the bereaved woman said a very disturbing thing, "Most of these people never shared Bob's faith, and now they don't know what to say. Death frightens them and brings this fear out into the open. How can I communicate to them that Bob is alive?"

Many of us are like those friends. We try to cover the stark reality of death with sentimental substitutes. I sat next to a man on an airplane. We fell into the typical conversation about weather, the stock market, and politics, when suddenly an anxious pall fell over his face. He was obviously very angry at himself. "I constantly forget to take out insurance before I fly," he explained. "Then I sit through the flight wondering about my wife and kids."

The fear of a crash was very deep within him. He was alarmed by what his death would do to his family. As Charles Dickens said, it is a disquieting thing to do anything for the last time.

Fortified by a couple of those things flight attendants serve before dinner, he talked at length about death and his own uncertainty about what he believed. Many of us share his concerns but seldom bring them out into the open. A creative, in-depth conversation about life and death is a rare experience.

In one church I served, the session introduced a program to promote a more Christian observation of the fact of death. In order to be able to follow our people's wishes for their memorial services more sensitively, we asked each member to fill out a form indicating preferences for their memorial witness. They could designate their desires for hymns, and meaningful Scriptures, clarify the causes friends could contribute to in their memory, and indicate a desire to dedicate their remains for the service of science. The information was invaluable for more effectively communicating the hope of the person at the time of his death.

What amazed me was the tumult of emotion this created. Some spouses actually hid the questionnaires for fear of the anxiety it would create in the psyches of their loved ones. Others did some very creative thinking about death and the future. I remember the remarkable rise in my counseling on the subject. One man whose initial reaction was hostility said to me, "When I cooled down, I realized I was angry about death itself. Since my wife and I have talked about it, I find that I am not sure about eternal life for myself or my loved ones. I have never faced the idea of death for myself."

There is a deep unease in many of us about death. We postpone thinking about it until our busy lives are interrupted with its stark reality by the death of a close friend or loved one. The question is there but seldom faced: "How do I feel about my own death?"

Will you join me in an honest experiment? Will you let your thoughts and emotions go for a moment and direct them to this triangular question: "If I were to die this week, would it be the end of everything, a transition in living, or the beginning of a new and triumphant life?"

Are you ready to die? I don't mean are you fed up with life, but how sure do you feel about death? What longings would be left unexperienced, unexpressed, and unfulfilled? What assurance do you have that you will live forever? If this were your midnight hour when we all must unmask, where do you think you would spend eternity? Must you hold your emotions tightly in check for fear they will begin to reveal the anguish you really have about dying?

The real question is: On which side of Easter are you living? Are you on the dark, dreary, defeated side, where the powers of evil still reign and death still has the final word? Or are you living on the blessed, beautiful side of the resurrection, with an assurance that Christ has won, death has been defeated, and eternal life has begun in a way that no mere cessation of physical life can hinder?

Jesus Christ said, "I am the resurrection and the life; he who lives and believes in me shall never die." But he followed this profound statement with a penetrating question: "Do you believe this?" (John 11:25).

What does the Easter parade mean to you personally? A procession of pageantry? A symphony of words and song? The cross-shaped symmetry of flowers and decorations? The fuzzy sentimentalism of bunnies and eggs? What difference does the fact of Christ's resurrection mean to you? Has it changed your attitude about death? About the kind of life you live and the hopes you cherish?

The historical evidence of the fact of Easter—the real Easter parade—is the procession of liberated, loving, laughing men and women who march triumphantly across the pages of the New Testament in an abandoned quality of life. Their fear of death has been discharged. The procession moves exultantly through the pages of history to our own day.

The grim reaper has rapped at the door of their emotions and has been turned away, rejected. The thrill of victory is in their hearts, hope is their banner, and their chant resounds, "Christ is risen! He is risen indeed! Hallelujah!" Death has been faced and conquered for them. They are alive because Christ is alive. The early Christian hymn is sung boldly, "Not Christ, but death died yesternight!"

The procession beckons us to join the celebration. Resurrection is not only for Jesus in Joseph's garden. Through him, it is for each one of us today.

One triumphant word strikes an octave in all these texts I have selected from the treasure chest of great Scripture classics about the hope of the resurrection. That word is victory.

Paul's treatise on the resurrection in 1 Corinthians 15 reaches a climactic crescendo. His thoughts soar in fantastic rhetoric. He has explained the triumphant fact that Jesus Christ has done battle with the powers of evil. The Cross was more than a planetary event. It was a cosmic conflict and Christ has won! It was God himself who came in Jesus Christ. The life he lived was so filled with power that the resurrection followed as naturally as day follows night.

The idea of recapitulation is basic in Paul's thought here. Jesus was the new Adam—the beginning of a new creation. "As in (the old) Adam all die, so also in Christ (the new Adam) shall all be made alive" (verse 22). For Paul, that meant that those who were in Christ were recipients of his love and forgiveness, those in whom Christ had become living Lord—and the same victory over death experienced by Christ would be theirs.

Death is powerless over that quality of life.

The great truth is that the same transcendent life

dwells in us. We were meant for eternal existence, not merely a quantity of time but a quality of life. When we believe in Christ—die to our own will, surrender our rebellion and independence—we are lifted to that new level of life. The intrinsic death of a Christian occurs long before his physical death. Eternal life is a life fully open to God, filled with his power, open to his direction. That's what Paul found and why he could sing the ancient lyrics with new vigor: "Death is swallowed up in victory! O death, where is thy sting?"

But Paul's essential conviction about death is still to follow. "The sting of death is sin," he says (verse 56). Sin, for Paul, was separation from God, hostility toward his guidance, self-will in rejection of his will, and pride in human adequacy. And finally, it was the sting of death. Death has power only over those who are not in a relationship of grace with God.

Paul continues, "The sting of death is sin, and the power of sin is the law." The law is symbolic of man's effort to be good enough through his own adequacy. Through the law, man had tried to order his life to fulfill God's justice. The result was self-oriented, ego-satisfying self-justification. Men had achieved everything but personal knowledge of God and that assurance which could only come through an experience of his forgiving love. "The power of sin is the law"—and now the alternative is clearly stated—"but thanks be to God who gives us the victory through our Lord Jesus Christ."

Victory! That is the key word of the resurrection. The undeniable faith of Paul and the early church was that Christ had won. His victory was their victory and the evidence of it was in their victorious lives. Confidence against death was the obvious result. The ethos one feels in the early church is an overwhelming resilience, an abounding vitality. These are people who had found the victory of a deathless life. They really believed they were alive forever!

Paul took a familiar passage from Hosea and looked at it fearlessly in the new light of the resurrection. Hosea had written, quoting the judgment of God upon the rebellion of ancient Israel, "Shall I ransom them from the power of Sheol? Shall I redeem them from Death? O Death, where are your plagues? O Sheol, where is your destruction? Compassion is hid from my eyes" (Hosea 13:14).

How different is the tone of the Apostle's evocative sequel addressed to the Corinthians. God *had* taken compassion on his people. In Christ, death *had* had its power. "O death, where is thy victory?" Death is swallowed up in victory!

The fear of the ages has been met. Jesus Christ has come to liberate us from death's debilitating anguish. To break the bonds of death. To throw wide the gate of the tomb and make it possible for us to arise to an eternal dimension of life. We do not need to spend our days in morbid worry or in frantically crushing the substance of life into the brief years of mortal existence.

The sword of Damocles has been removed!

Paul Tillich said that death is the secret anxiety of modern men and women. We all feel it rumbling beneath the surface. We are beguiled by what Rudolph Otto called the "tremendous mystery." But the Apostle Paul said, "Lo! I tell you a mystery. We shall all be changed... The dead will be raised imperishable, and we shall be changed" (15:51, 52).

Christ said: "Because I live, ye shall live also." Do you believe that? Faith is our response to his offer of love, our joyous acceptance of the gift offered in the resurrection. Faith says "yes" and allows you, through obedience, to live in Christ's resurrection power and under his marching orders. The resurrection fact makes possible resurrected living. The secret is this: Those who have faced and conquered death are alive in a totally different dimension of life.

The Spirit of the living Christ invades our lives and begins what Keats called "the vale of soul making"— the refashioning of us into his own likeness. That's the joy and challenge of daily living—being groomed by Christ to live forever!

Archbishop William Temple proclaimed: "The stress of the New Testament ... does not call men to a mere survival of death while they remain very much what they were before, but to a resurrection, to a new order of being of which the chief characteristic is fellowship with God."

The message of the resurrection and the promise of the Lord's Table are the same. They meet us at the point of our deepest needs. They give us the courage to face the evil powers of death and know without fear that it no longer has power over us. Not only do they speak of endless life, but of a life of endless victory.

It is the victory of joy over unhappiness, of fellowship over loneliness, of honesty over moral pride and self-deception, of purity over lust, of truth over error, of love over hatred. We cannot overcome the things which beset us by our own power, but we shall win by the victory of Christ.

Think what this means for the habits which bind us. The attitudes which cripple us. The fears which limit us. Bring them out into the open. Acknowledge their power. Allow the resurrected Lord to meet them and to do battle against them in us as we take the bread and raise the cup.

This introduces the final great word which is an aspect of the true victory the resurrection makes possible. It is closely related to power to overcome, but stresses the source of that power. The author of Hebrews says: "Since therefore the children share in flesh and blood, he himself likewise partook of the same nature, that through death he might destroy him who has the power of death ... and deliver all those who through fear of death were subject to lifelong bondage" (2:14, 15). We are delivered from bondage by the resurrection. Lifelong fear of death can be healed, and we can live a deathless life.

The amazing fact is that the more we contemplate the meaning of death, the more we will live our lives now. In his book *A Doctor Looks at Death*, Dr. Felix Marti-Ibanez says, "The man who loves life lives a fuller and better life because he has put death into its proper place."

Death sensitizes us to life. It forces us to grapple with basic issues. It is in knowing how to die that a man most perfectly lives all the rest of his life.

When troubled Israel repented of their sin in the wilderness, God took the symbol of their death, a fiery serpent, and lifted it up and made it a symbol of life. At the Last Supper, Jesus Christ took the symbol of death, his broken body, and made it a symbol of a totally different dimension of life.

As we take the bread and the cup, let us eat and drink to life!

15

How to Get It All Together

2 Corinthians 13:14;
Acts 2:44

I would like to borrow a contemporary phrase and propose that the Communion Service can be an experience of "getting it all together."

When you put a slightly different emphasis on that phrase which implies that your heart and mind and body are all coordinated, it is amazing what it can mean.

I want to offer a promise to you that this can be our contemporary Pentecost here today. That we can receive all God has to give—and that we can get it all together.

Paul finished his letter to the Christians at Corinth with a benediction that sounds oddly like the worship of three gods instead of one. He said: "The grace of the Lord Jesus Christ ... the love of God ... and the fellowship of the Holy Spirit be with you all." We begin to wonder, do we have Jesus Christ here, God the Father here, and the Holy Spirit here?

A similar question could be raised when we talk

about our faith. We talk about God as a distinct entity, the Holy Spirit as some kind of mystical essence, and then Jesus Christ as a personal friend. What we end up with in Protestantism often is a tritheism that debilitates the oneness of God.

The Apostle Paul was not giving a theology of the Trinity here. Rather he was giving facets of the experience of God which the Corinthian church had known. He drew their minds back to the essential experience of what God had meant to them. God was indeed a father to them. Because of what Jesus Christ had revealed of the nature of God, they could come to call him their Father.

The center of their experience of God was through the Cross, where his loving, accepting, unmerited favor was real to them in Jesus Christ. And so they could say, "May the grace of the Lord Jesus be with you."

Then, indicating the intimacy and empowering of God, they could speak of the communion (KJV), the *koinonia*, the sharing and participation in the living Spirit of God.

They knew nothing of three Gods. They knew something of a great God who had created the world, who had dwelt in Jesus Christ, and who was with them in the power of the Holy Spirit.

I wonder why we live as such paupers when all of the power of God has been offered to us? I hear Christians say, "I believed once, but I don't seem to have the energy to follow through on what I believe. Christ doesn't seem as real any more. There was a time when I knew him intimately and with power. Now he's aloof and I can't seem to reach him."

How to Get It All Together

I want to suggest that the most desperate need in our life is for a contemporary Pentecost. I believe that what those Apostles needed, we need right now.

The need I recognize in you is in myself. I need a God who is not far away. Not a God of theory or theological formulation. Not a God that I can observe in the strength of other Christians, but a God who takes possession of me. Who gives me the same power and capacity he gave those apostles and that first colony of Christians to move out and change the world.

I do not need to believe more. I already believe more than I can understand. I don't need to know more about my obligations and responsibilities. I already know how short I fall. What I need is a lifting power. A driving power. A power from within that will enable me to live the life that Christ has suggested is possible.

"Grandpa, what's the wind?" the child asked.

"I can't explain the wind to you," the old fisherman replied, "but I can teach you how to raise your sail!"

I believe that's what Pentecost Sunday is all about. A signal to raise a sail. Catch the wind. To help us recognize that the living God, the Lord of all, wants to enter into a deep, energizing, and intimate relationship with every one of us. You see, our nature is not only physical, not only soul, but also spirit.

It is because of the ministry of the Holy Spirit that we were able to respond initially and give our lives to Christ. He came within us and convinced us of the efficacy of Christ in the gospel. It was then that he began his work within us.

Pentecost is not so much the power of God coming from outside of us to immerse us, but the power of God answering from within us—bursting forth and inundating every dimension of our being. Pentecost is the power of God within us flowing into the tissues and fibres of our minds. Drenching the memory factors of our emotions. Cleansing and freeing us to love and care. Giving us healing and wholeness and strength.

From within you shall flow rivers of living water, Jesus Christ said (John 7:38). From the day you said "yes" to the Holy Spirit, he has been at work in your life. Moving in you. Growing in you. Developing in you so that this might be your Pentecost. So that like those apostles of old who had everything they needed except power, we too might cry out for the power only he can give.

The communion of the Holy Spirit, however, is not just my separate experience. I get it—we get it—all together. And it is only as I am related to you that I am able to receive the power of the Holy Spirit. It was when those apostles loved each other utterly, were gathered together in that upper room caring for each other without reservation—it was only as the barriers were lifted from between them that the Holy Spirit gripped them.

You can't get it all alone. You get it all in *koinonia*, in the communion of the Holy Spirit.

That's the reason as we pass the tray to each other we say simply, "This is the body of the Lord Jesus broken for you." We become in that moment a priest to another person and offer to be broken bread to that person. As we take the cup and share it, we promise to pour ourselves out to that person.

Communion takes you—you can't take communion.

And when it does you are gripped and uplifted by it. Suddenly we know that Pentecost has come.

Would you hear the rushing of the wind? Would you feel the fire of Pentecost upon your head? I wonder if it wouldn't also come as a deep inner assurance. A new capacity to love and care. I wonder if we wouldn't be galvanized with the realization that we are indeed one as we experience the power of the Holy Spirit.

The Spirit of God is here. In us and amongst us as we experience the communion of the Holy Spirit. He wants more than anything else in this moment for us to get it all together.

Amen.

16
Come Home

John 14:1-3, 6, 15, 23;
2 Corinthians 5:6-9, 16

Ian Maclaren has distinguished himself in his great Scottish stories. He tells a delightful tale of Lackland Campbell and his daughter Dora.

Dora left home and fell into the wrong kind of relationships. She began to misuse the gifts of life. Soon she did not respond to her father's letters because she found it difficult to relate to him.

Maggie, Dora's aunt, wrote her a letter that finally melted her heart. Next to the words of our Lord, the last words of that letter comprise the most poignant, the most magnificent invitation to Holy Communion that I have ever read. At the end of the letter Maggie writes:

"Dora, your Daddy is a grievin' ye. Come home for your own sake. Come home for your dear Daddy's sake. But, Dora, come home most of all for the dear Lord's sake!"

The invitation to Holy Communion is simply the invitation to come home.

Come Home

Softly and tenderly Jesus is calling. Calling for you and for me. Come home ... come home ... come home.

John described the Incarnation very simply. He said, "He came to his own home, and his own people received him not" (John 1:11, RSV).

Now the term John uses for the word *home* is the same word that's used for mansion. It's the very same word that's used in Greek to translate Jesus' words: "In my Father's house are many mansions." Jesus went to prepare a place for us which will be our eternal home. Meanwhile, he said, "The Father and I shall come and make our home in you."

"When I am in the body," the Apostle Paul said, "I am away from the Lord. I long to go home to the Lord." And yet as you study the context of his writing and couple it with Paul's whole message, you recognize the gripping nowness of what he has said. "The old has passed away, behold the new has come. Now is the acceptable time" (2 Cor. 5:17; 6:2).

I believe that the thrust of that passage is that there is a quality of relationship with the living God that is like truly being at home!

And it begins now. We know that our death shall be no more feared than our bed at night. That our dying shall be no more than a transition in our living. That our going home will be secure because we have been at home with the Lord during the days of our life.

Home is not a place. It's a person. Who hasn't discovered that? Home is not a position, not an address with a mortgage. Home is a passion. Home is where the heart is and the heart is where Jesus Christ is.

Softly and tenderly Jesus is calling. Come home. Right now. Come home to him!

Take the letters of the word sin and you get an acrostic that takes you to the very heart of the theological meaning of the nature of sin. Sin is separation, independence, and negativism.

Sin is separation from God. It is to be independent and to want to run your own life. It is to be negative about the amazing potentials—the unbelievable surprises of God waiting serendipitously in every day.

To be a sinner—and none of us likes that word or likes to be identified with it—is to be one who in any part of his life is separated from God. One who in any quarter of his life is trying to go it alone. With clenched fists. With knuckles white.

To be a sinner is to be one who cannot appropriate the amazing power that God has offered.

Now I suggest that there are many people who, like the prodigal son, are away from home. Some of us are away because we have never known what a home is like. We've never met the Savior. We have never known that gracious, accepting, forgiving, empowering love.

But there are others who do know him and still live in a sort of quasi-exile because there are areas of their lives not under his control. The closer you get to him, the more you realize that there are little insurrections in areas of your life that make it difficult for you to take the pure Christ-symbols of bread and wine into your being. You say, "I'm not worthy. With the kind of life I've lived, I shouldn't even be here."

And the memories flood in. And the uncertain plans are exposed. And the broken relationships ache and hurt.

And then there are those who have both met him and know him. They have moved close enough to him to have discovered something of the nature of God. They have seen the door into eternity begin to swing open and suddenly their little souls are satiated. The people who know all there is to know and have all of the answers topically and hermetically sealed for instant access have never really come face to face with the magnificent, living Lord.

To know him is to know that you have barely begun to grow.

I suggest that we need to come home in all the areas of our lives—from all the alternatives of our lives, from our sealed, esoteric faith, away from the attitudes which have led to the atomizing of life—and find the Savior. Every time we come to the Table we are reminded of things we've done and said. Wouldn't it be wonderful to have an experience that would once and for all take those things that make us uneasy in the presence of the Lord, take them to him in a prayer of confession and commitment and destroy their power?

I can remember a breakfast in a downtown club in Chicago with a very sophisticated group of leaders of the business community. We were having an informal communion. We just took some bread and some grape juice and before we began I said to the men, "Write down the thing in your memory that always comes to your mind when you take communion."

Highly polished gold-plated pens went to work immediately. There wasn't one in that room who did not have something to put down. I took that pile of folded memories, put them together, and lit a match to them. As we watched them curl and char, I said, "My brothers, in the name of Jesus Christ, you are forgiven!"

> Softly and tenderly Jesus is calling. Come home. Come home.

What are the unresolved questions and fears in our lives that keep us from coming home to God? The turgid, turbulent inner thoughts that lurk at the edge of our subconscious and draw energy off our being? What are the alienating feelings and the attitudes that make it difficult for us to be in relationship with our living Lord?

As one great man said, "There seems to be a tapestry between the Lord and me. I hear him calling but I can't see him. I don't sense his reality because there's something between the two of us." What stolen, contraband threads weave together the tapestry of your rebellion? What in your life makes it difficult to see his magnificent face and feel his present power?

And what are the plans for the future? What have you planned without consulting him? Do you find yourself marooned somewhere between tomorrow's hopes and yesterday's scrapbook?

He'll give you strength to support anything that's in character with his nature in you. The strategy of the

Come Home

Christian is to be so close to him that he's already willed the power for the things we plan and do.

Many of us are in far countries of broken relationships. Far countries of criticism. Far countries of settled opinions where we have placed people in the category of our own intransigent judgment and left them there. And Jesus is saying, "Leave that judgment in the far country and come home to me. Let me give you a new relationship with that person as you come to my table."

Softly and tenderly, Jesus is calling!

Unless I miss my guess, many of us have known the pain of spoken and unspoken words. We approach the Table with a little bit of uneasiness—a little bit of strangeness. Good marriages could well become our rarest works of art, someone has said, because character and selflessness are required in such large doses.

There are parents whose effort at shaping and molding their children has met with futility and rebellion. And there are children whose relationships with their parents are filled with a combination of love and hostility.

Jesus says, "Let me take that." "Stop playing God." "Let me forgive that." "Let me help you dismantle those walls." "Let me cleanse your spirit and give you a new beginning."

A man came to my office who had been away from home for three weeks. He felt he couldn't go home because of the things he had said and done. After we talked for a long time, I called his wife and asked, "Fran, would you like your husband to come home?"

131

She answered, "On what terms?"

I talked to her about her judgments. Her wounded feelings. Her husband. When he picked up the telephone some minutes later, he heard something which sounded very much like what Maggie said to Dora:

"John, come home. Come home for the children's sake. Come home for my sake. And come home because God loves you." He put down the phone and said, "I'm going home!"

Softly and tenderly Jesus is calling!

When the sailors took the body of Admiral Nelson and carried it high into the cathedral, it was draped with a magnificent Union Jack. Later they carried it to the graveside. When the body was being lowered down, almost as if there had been a whistle from an unseen quarterdeck, each one of those sailors who had served with the Admiral took hold of the flag and ripped it apart. "I've got a piece of him," they said, "and I'll never forget him."

We've got a piece of him and we'll never forget him!

He anticipated our need for this sacramental identification when he broke the bread and blessed the cup. He said, "Do this in remembrance of me."

> *We come to the Table, O God. We've been away from home. You are our only security and peace. We reach for you. We long for you. We want you. We come for our own sakes. We come for the sake of those who have prayed for us and modeled your love. But most of all, we come for the dear Lord's sake. Amen.*

17
The Wine of Astonishment

Psalm 60:3;
Mark 1:22

There are times when I read the Scriptures, trying to get hold on their meaning, that I come across a phrase which gets a hold on me. My own needs, the concerns of the people whom I lead as a pastor, and the conditions of the times in which we live strike on the flint of an eternal truth, and I am set on fire with a new insight which burns like a wildfire across the dry fields of my imagination.

That happened to me one day when I was reading Psalm 60 in the King James Version. My eye paused at the third verse. I had never seen the phrase the way I did that day. I was anticipating a service of communion at the Lord's Table and had asked our Lord for a fresh insight to share in this meditation. What he gave was a new excitement for what the sacrament can mean to all of us.

There it was. The words leaped off the page. "Thou hast made us to drink the wine of astonishment." What an impelling image for the cup of the new covenant!

THE CUP OF WONDER

The wine of communion, the sacramental element of the crushed grape, is the wine of astonishment for us. Christ's blood was shed for us. We are astonished, indeed, by the depth of love, the gift of forgiveness and reconciliation, and the intervening power of his Spirit infused within us for the facing of the circumstances of our lives.

My mind quickly sped to the original Hebrew words the King James Version had translated and then to the context of this spellbinding phrase. I found that the Hebrew roots of the words meant, "wine of staggering" or "wine of agitation." The Revised Standard Version translates it, "Thou hast given us wine to drink that made us reel." Astonishment in the Old Testament is a reaction to the acts of God. Often it is stirred by the judgment of God or some event which caused the response of surprise, wonder, and awe. But dread is also a part of astonishment. *The Living Bible* translation of our text emphasizes, "You have been very hard on us and made us reel beneath your blows."

The word "astonished" had captured my attention. I thought of the response to Jesus' teaching and healing in the synagogue in Capernaum. "And they were astonished at his teaching, for he taught them as one who had authority, and not as the scribes." The Greek word for astonished, *ekplēssō*, used here and elsewhere in the Gospels to describe the reaction of the people after hearing the message and witnessing the acts of Jesus, means "to strike out, expel by a blow, drive out or away; to strike a person out of self-possession." It describes prolonged amazement, stirring impact.

That's exactly what happened to people who came in

contact with Jesus. They were driven out of themselves and their careful containment. He spoke about God with firsthand experience and knowledge. He did not quote authorities, he had authority. He did not quibble about regulations but communicated a relationship with God. He was filled with God's Spirit and every fiber of his being mediated love and hope. The people's astonishment was because they had never heard anyone speak and act the way Jesus did. Nor have we. Our vital encounter with the living God as he comes to us in the Savior at communion breaks open our reserve, blasts us free from resistance, and bursts the chains of the prison of self-imposed fear.

In that light, I returned to Psalm 60 to meditate on the wine of astonishment as the gift which is given when we experience communion.

The context of the total Psalm was equally rewarding as my mind grappled with this amazing phrase. God had gained the Psalmist's attention through a series of emotional calamities. A shattering national defeat had awakened him out of the slumbers of complacency, and he was forced to see God's judgment in what was happening. He was not simplistic in his view of tragedy as the chance fatalism of meaningless forces over which he had no control. The Psalmist was a God-sensitized man who faced difficulties in himself and his nation and asked, "Lord, what are you trying to tell me and your people?" He knew God was in charge and did not equivocate with an evasive, "If it hadn't been for that, or them, or me!"

Instead, he listened for what God had to say and what he wanted to have happen to his people through what was happening to them. And what he heard was the experience of the heady wine of astonishment. There is a progression in his astonishing realization: God's judgment, God's intervention, and God's ultimate victory for his people. The wine of communion is all three for us.

We are astonished by the blood of the Cross. It startles us with the realization of how seriously God takes sin. It's rebellion, self-justification, separation from him, and disruption of his plan and purpose for us. It's the running of our own lives that eventually, irreversibly runs our lives amuck. From our sin of separation from him come all the little sins of selfishness and pride that twist our own natures, starve the people around us for love, and confuse our daily lives.

When we catch a vision of what God intended life to be—dependent on him, surrendered to his will, and filled with his Spirit—then we can focus the nature of our sin. The rupture of our relationship with him makes us the selfish, anxious, compulsive people we are. All because we refuse to allow him to love us and fail to accept his unlimited grace!

Only a Cross could astonish us! Only a love like the Son of God's could blast us out of our self-erected incarceration. Frankly, I am astonished that it would take that for me. T. S. Eliot was right, "Our age is an age of moderate virtue and of moderate vice." It is so difficult for us to see and admit our need! The wine of the communion confronts us. We cannnot take it lightly or with ceremonial uninvolvement. To take the cup is to take the cup of salvation. That's radical. It's saying, "Lord, you died for me! My sin and sins made it necessary! Forgive me, Lord!" Then we can say with W. M. Gregor, "Thou has made us and we are Thine; Thou hast redeemed us and we are doubly Thine."

But that must be rediscovered in every circumstance, problem, and tension. The Psalmist was astonished, after what he and his people had done, that God would still persist to help them. Who wouldn't be astonished?

> Thou hast set up a banner for those who fear
> thee....
> That thy beloved may be delivered.

Oh, to be God's beloved! That's the source of amazement, inexpressible joy, astonishment which blasts us open in incredulous delight. It's one thing to know that we have failed and been forgiven, but to go on compulsively, repetitiously, intentionally to do those things which break God's heart and still be "beloved" is so far beyond our barter concept of love that we find it difficult to appropriate. That's why we need the wine of astonishment repeatedly and often. We forget so easily. No wonder Jesus said, "Do this in remembrance of me."

J. S. Whale once said that we "take photographs of the burning bush from suitable angles instead of taking off our shoes because we are on holy ground." We do that at the Lord's Table. Everything's fastidiously crisp and clean, laundered and starched, pleasant and beautiful. But there's a burning bush that's not consumed on this Table. It's the cup of our Lord, filled with the blood of a sacrifice for you and me. We need not only to take off our shoes, but to open our minds and hearts. We are the Lord's "beloved" and that means that forgiveness and a new beginning is but a repentant prayer away.

That's what galvanizes us together around the Lord's Table. Our astonishment enables acceptance of each other. "Real fellowship," says Jamie Buckingham, "is ... coming together like grapes ... crushed ... knowing each other's sins and failures and weaknesses ... with skins of ego broken ... the rich, fragrant, exhilarating juices of life mingling with the wine of sharing, understanding, accepting, forgiving, and caring. Fellowship is the fusing of personalities in the Presence and Person of Jesus Christ."

After we read the opening lines of Psalm 60, we feel the jig is up; man finally did the thing which would make God stop loving him. Not so! There's a banner for those who fear him. It's a Cross! Why? That his beloved may be delivered.

John Buchan once said, "An atheist is a man with no invisible means of support." Clever rhetoric! But we are God's "beloved" and the invisible means of support are visible here before us. Bread: A broken body for us. Wine: A Savior's blood shed in our place for what we have been and done.

That should be enough to astonish us. But the Psalmist is not only amazed at God's judgment and forgiveness, or even that his love persists through repeated rejection, but that he intervenes to help his people. He is free to pray, "O grant us help against the foe, for vain is the help of man!" That is a prayer for specific help in daily battles in which neither our own strength nor the assistance of others is adequate.

The Wine of Astonishment

Communion is an astonishing experience because it
enables us to see God at work in all of life. We commune with him now in order that all of life will be a
successive series of astonishments with what God is
able and ready to do through intervening love. Jesus'
"Lo, I am with you always" becomes the basis of a
sensitized recognition of his breakthrough into our
problems. When we least expect it, he is there. When
we are not aware of his presence, he gives us what we
need. There are times when the language of the old
gospel song alone suffices, "Hallelujah! What a Savior!"

Suddenly all of life is alive with the Holy Spirit. What
we need is what Newman called a "wise receptivity,"
yet many of us who participate in communion will not
be in communion with our Lord during the next week.

I have come to believe that an outward evidence of
the indwelling of the Holy Spirit is the capacity to be
constantly astonished at what God is up to in our lives.
A bored, bland, unsurprisable, unamazed Christian is
a contradiction of terms. My prayer is, "O God, keep
me sensitive to see you alive in the world around me,
active in the lives of people, and abundant in unexpected blessings."

Saul Kane expressed that kind of astonishment after
his conversion in John Masefield's poem "The Everlast-
ing Mercy."

> The station brook, to my new eyes
> Was babbling out of Paradise.
> The waters rushing from the rain
> Were singing Christ has risen again.

THE CUP OF WONDER

I thought all earthly creatures knelt
From rapture of the joy I felt.[1]

But the cup of astonishment is not yet empty. There is one further draught for our thirsty souls. If we sipped the wine of judgment and forgiveness, drank the wine of limitless love, gulped the wine of intervening grace, it is now time to empty the cup and experience the last drops of the wine of final victory. "With God we shall do valiantly" is the settled confidence of the Psalmist. That's the triumphant faith of draining the cup.

It is astonishing, isn't it, that all the enemies in life and death have been defeated through Jesus Christ's life and death. Fear of any eventuality, even our own death, can not destroy us. He has done all things to set us free to live the abundant life.

An authentic experience of communion deals with all dimensions of past, present, and future. What's done is forgiven; what's now is given power; what is to be will be dealt with valiantly. The future is ablaze with yet undiscovered evidence of his grace.

Now we can empathize with the enthusiasm the apostles felt after Pentecost. The experience of the Holy Spirit burst forth in a joy that made the leaders of Israel say that they were drunk with new wine. "They stood there amazed and perplexed. 'What can this mean?' they asked each other. But others in the crowd were mocking. 'They're drunk, that's all!' they said. Then Peter stepped forward with the eleven apostles, and

---

[1] John Masefield, *Poems* (New York: Macmillian, 1930), p. 80.

shouted to the crowd, 'Listen, all of you, visitors and residents of Jerusalem alike! Some of you are saying these men are drunk! It isn't true! It's much too early for that! People don't get drunk by 9 A.M.! No! What you see this morning was predicted centuries ago by the prophet Joel—"In the last days," God said, "I will pour out my Holy Spirit upon all mankind" ' " (Acts 2:12-17, TLB).

The experience of God's Son as Messiah and Lord, the witness of his loving death and appearances giving them assurance, had now been maximized by the experience of his indwelling Spirit. No wonder their joy was mistaken for drunkenness. They had emptied the cup of salvation. They were filled with the wine of astonishment.

If a stranger walked in upon our communion celebration, would he be forced to explain our joy by saying that we were filled with new wine? Should not our delight, warmth, and love be that exhilarating? Only astonished Christians will ever amaze the world.

Have you ever been astonished at communion? Has faithless familiarity or commonness of custom robbed you of being driven out of yourself in an experience of sheer amazement? I pray that what happened to Proconsul Sergius Paulus when Barnabas and Paul communicated the power of the gospel, might be our communion. *The Living Bible* translation of Acts 13:12 is very impelling. "When the governor saw what happened he believed and was astonished at the power of God's message." I ask God for nothing less for all of us as we grasp the cup and are astonished out of ourselves and into limitless joy. It's time to celebrate!